31 DAYS to a clutter free LIFE

ONE MONTH to clear your HOME, MIND & SCHEDULE

RUTH SOUKUP

ISBN: 0692252711
ISBN 13: 9780692252710

31 Days to a Clutter-Free Life
One Month to Clear your Home, Mind & Schedule

Ruth Soukup
www.LivingWellSpendingLess.com

Table of Contents

Introduction

Life is busy and sometimes hectic and often very, very full. Full of obligations, full of things to remember, full of paperwork and bills to pay, full of things to put away and stuff to manage.

There are times where it all just feels like too much to handle. We know, deep down, something needs to give, and yet we can't quite seem to slow down long enough to step back, reassess, and take back our lives from the clutter that is weighing us down.

Sometimes we just need someone else to walk us through the process of de-cluttering our lives, to break down what seems like an impossible task into manageable bites that we can tackle one day at a time.

This is that book.

The purpose of this book is not to overwhelm you with information, but to give you a practical, step-by-step guide to clearing your home, your mind, and your schedule of the excess clutter that tends to pile up.

Each day we will focus on one small area of our homes and lives, knowing that together these small tweaks will add up to a big change. To keep it manageable, each assignment is short and to the point. There are also some handy worksheets and checklists for you to use, in case you are like me and prefer to check things off a list to feel like you have actually accomplished something. (There is a link to download a printable version of the checklists located at the end of this book.)

It may not always be fun or easy, but I can promise that it will be worth the effort.

Finally, as you complete each day's challenge, share your successes on Instagram, Facebook, and Twitter with the hashtag #LWSLClutterFree. For more moral support and to share ideas and encouragement you can also join the 31 Days to a Clutter Free Life forum thread found at www.LWSLEveryday.com.

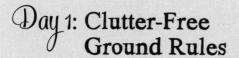

Day 1: Clutter-Free Ground Rules

The older I get, the more STUFF I seem to accumulate, and the more desperately I long to live a life free of clutter. While I don't think I will ever be considered a minimalist, I dream of a home that is pared down to just the essentials—only those things I love and use on a regular basis. I dream of order and organization and simplicity, of fewer things and less stress, and of more meaning and greater purpose.

And so I thought it was time to take on a new challenge:

31 Days to a Clutter-Free Life.

Do you want to join me?

In this challenge we will be giving ourselves one month to scale back on all the things we no longer want or need. One month to purge the excess and to instead create a home that fosters balance and harmony. One month to simplify the chaos and calm the storm that comes with always having too much stuff.

I'm ready. In fact, I'm *more* than ready!

Are you?

Then let's get started!

1

Every challenge needs a few ground rules, so before we dive right in, I think it is essential that we establish some firm guidelines for how to tackle the clutter we find throughout our space.

Challenge Requirements:

- **Everything must have a home**—Clutter most often piles up because we don't know where to put it, so it goes to follow that one of the biggest keys to conquering clutter is ensuring that every object has a home.

- **Everything must have a purpose**—Too often we keep things because they were a gift, or because they were expensive, or because we feel like we have to. The truth is that keeping items in our life that have no purpose just gives us more to do. Instead, we will adhere to the rule made famous by William Morris: Keep nothing in your homes that you don't know to be useful or believe to be beautiful.

- **Everything must be in good working order**—The fact of the matter is that if it doesn't work it is time to either fix it or let it go. Broken items only add additional stress and chaos to our lives.

- **Everything must have a label**—It might seem like overkill at first, but labels allow not only US to know where things go, but let everyone else know as well. In a family, this is pretty essential. Once we give our items a home, we must give their homes a label as well. This makes it real.

- **If it needs to go, get it out FAST**—When things sit around in a box in the garage, they inevitably make their way back into your home and your life. As soon as you clear a space, make sure to finish the job and actually get the clutter out of your home by donating it to charity, bringing it to a consignment shop, or selling it on Craigslist, Facebook, or eBay.

How to Prepare:

1. **Prepare your mind.** Mentally commit to the process of letting things go. Realize that things will not improve unless you are ready to make some serious changes, and that those changes may at times be a little painful.

2. **Prepare your family.** Let your spouse and children know that change is coming and that you plan to drastically purge the clutter that is currently weighing you down. Let your kids know that if they have things they don't want to lose, they will need to find a home for them. Discuss with your spouse what kind of changes you are both comfortable with so that you are on the same page. Keep your family as involved with the process as you can.

3. **Prepare your schedule.** Reserve 30-60 minutes each day this month to focus on this challenge and to complete your assignment. Block out even more time on the weekends to get caught up and to sell or donate any items you are getting rid of.

4. **Prepare your supplies.** Gather the items you will need to complete your assignments—boxes for collecting the items you plan to get rid of, a camera for taking photos of the things you plan to sell, and a label maker for labeling everything. You may also need to collect some practical storage bins or containers, but it is generally better to figure out exactly what you need for a particular area first.

5. **Prepare your space.** It is generally more motivating and less overwhelming to de-clutter when you start with a rela-

tively clean space. While it might not always be possible, try to start with a quick speed-cleaning session each day, or, at the very least, make sure your dishes are done, your counters are clear, and the general mess has been tidied.

Don't forget, as you complete each day's challenge, to share your successes or your "before" and "after" photos on Instagram, Facebook, and Twitter with the hashtag #LWSLClutterFree. For more moral support and to share ideas and encouragement you can also join the 31 Days to a Clutter Free Life forum thread found at www.LWSLEveryday.com.

$\mathcal{D}ay$ 2: Entryway

What better place to start our challenge than at the first place we see when we walk in? I don't know how it works in your home, but that area right inside our front door tends to be the dumping ground for *everything*—shoes, purses, backpacks, umbrellas, lunchboxes, school papers, random toys and pretty much anything else that comes through our door. Thus, it is a little disheartening to walk inside and immediately see a pile of clutter!

Today's assignment will help clear the clutter that tends to pile up in this zone and instead help create a clear, organized, and super-functional space that sets the standard for a clutter-free home.

Objective: A clear entryway that sets the tone for the rest of the home.

Assess the space: What needs to stay, what needs to go? Do we use it here? Does it have a home here? Is this the most convenient space for this object to stay?

Assignment:

1. **Clear the unnecessary**-Get rid of anything that does not belong in this area or add to the functionality of this area.

2. **Create space for the necessary:**
   - **Shoes/Boots**—consider using a pretty shoe rack, baskets, or boot tray to store and contain the shoes or boots that tend to collect in this area.
   - **Coats**—make sure the coat closet is free and clear of clutter and contains sturdy hangers for hanging coats. If there is not closet, provide sturdy hooks or a free-standing coat rack.
   - **Purses/Backpacks**—sturdy hooks on the wall or placed on the back of a coat closet door make ideal storage for purses and backpacks.
   - **Keys**—small hooks, a pretty bowl, or an actual key rack are perfect for eliminating misplaced keys.
   - **Umbrellas**—a pretty umbrella stand or even a tall, sturdy vase is ideal for storing umbrellas until you need them.
   - **Collection basket or baskets**—it is handy to have a basket or set of baskets right at the entry to store and collect any stray items that need to be put away.

ENTRYWAY INSPIRATION

Entryway Inspiration
1. Pretty entry with bench (BHG.com)
2. Family entry with numbered cubbies and hooks (HomeRemediesRX.com)
3. Entry with shoe storage, bench, and hooks (BHG.com)
4. Creating a pseudo-entry with coat rack and table (BHG.com)
5. Hall closet converted to entry (HouseofSmiths.com)

Day 2 Checklist:

- ☐ Take a "before" photo
- ☐ Clear the unnecessary—remove all items that don't belong
- ☐ Return items to their proper homes
- ☐ Sweep, dust, and vacuum this area
- ☐ Create a functional space for the necessary
  - Shoes/Boots
  - Coats
  - Purses/Backpacks
  - Keys
  - Umbrellas
  - Collection basket or baskets for things that need to be put away.
- ☐ Take an "after" photo and share on Instagram, Facebook, Pinterest, or Twitter with the hashtag #LWSLClutterFree!

Day 3: Mail

Paper clutter is a huge struggle for most families! Throughout this month we are going to work to create practical, easy-to-maintain systems for all of the different paperwork that finds its way into our lives. The first thing on the list? Mail!

There is unfortunately no good way to stop the onslaught of paper mail that continually pours into our homes. Thus the best way to keep all that mail clutter from getting out of control is to create a workable system that ensures no important letters in bill (literally) slip the cracks.

The system that seems to works best and be easiest to follow involves immediately dealing with junk mail by recycling it as soon as it comes through the door, while simultaneously collecting the important mail items in a central location to be dealt with at a regular day and time.

Objective: An easy-to follow system that ensures all mail is dealt with in a timely manner.

Assess the current situation: What is happening with mail right now? Where does it go? What are your habits? What are your biggest struggles?

Assignment:

1. **Gather and sort current mail into two piles**—keep and trash. Start your mail organization process by dealing with the mail that has already piled up. Immediately discard your trash pile, then spend time getting caught up on your "keep" items.

2. **Create a recycle station for immediately disposing of junk mail and catalogs.** A pretty bin just inside your front door is ideal, but you could also create a recycle station in the kitchen, laundry room, garage, or utility room. Just make sure it is someplace where you will use it!

3. **Unsubscribe from catalogs.** Spend an afternoon removing yourself from as many company mailing lists as possible. There is unfortunately no easy way to do this, but a phone call directly to each company should be sufficient.

4. **Create a collection bin or basket for remaining "real" mail.** Pick a pretty basket that can collect the mail you actually need to deal with. Put it in a convenient place where you will actually use it. For example, if your mail normally piles up on a particular counter in the kitchen, put the box or basket right on that counter.

5. **Designate a day/time each week to open and deal with mail.** Try to do it at the same time each week so that nothing slips through the cracks.

MAIL INSPIRATION

www.LivingWellSpendingLess.com

Photo Credits: Martha Stewart, Bright & Blithe, Live Simply by Annie, Pottery Barn

Mail Inspiration
1. Wire Mail Basket (LiveSimplybyAnnie.com)
2. Wall Hung Mail and Key Sorter (LiveSimplybyAnnie.com)
3. Fabric Mail Sorter (BrightandBlithe.wordpress.com)
4. Lid Rack Mail Sorter (MarthaStewart.com)
5. Daily Mail System and Organizer (PotteryBarn.com)

Day 3 Checklist:

☐ Take a "before" photo
☐ Gather and sort current mail into two piles—keep and trash.
☐ Create a recycle station for immediately disposing of junk mail and catalogs
☐ Unsubscribe from catalogs
☐ Create a collection bin or basket for "real" mail
☐ Designate a day/time each week to open and deal with mail
☐ On mail day, be sure to:
   • Open all mail
   • Respond to all mail that requires a response
   • Pay all bills and invoices
   • Add events to your calendar
☐ Take an "after" photo and share on Instagram, Facebook, Pinterest, or Twitter with the hashtag #LWSLClutterFree!

$\mathcal{D}ay$ 4: Living Room

Your living room, by definition, is the central hub of your home. It should be a room where everyone can come together, relax, play games, read, convene, hang out, and even watch television.

The living room should offer a space for each person in the household to relax. There should be plenty of seating, arranged in a way that encourages conversation, connections and family. There's a tendency to point all seating towards the television, but you should also consider the other more interactive activities that go on in your family's living room.

Display items in the room that represent who you are as a family and items that you truly love. Obey the rule that everything should be something you use or something you love. Knickknacks and trinkets should be pared down to the most important items—don't detract from them by letting them become dust collectors. Display them proudly, like a museum of your family's treasured artifacts.

Give new life to older and damaged items with a fresh coat of paint, a good cleaning, new pillows or pretty throw blankets. Toss out old magazines, paperwork and other items that pile up. Pare down knick knacks, books, and even furniture that you no longer use or that your family has outgrown—perhaps that old piano?

Old gaming consoles? Give these items new life by donating them to an afterschool program or to a charity. Give yourself permission to let go.

Objective: An open, comfortable, and inviting room for guests and family to gather, connect, and relax.

Assess the current situation: How is this room used right now? List all the purposes of this room. What are the biggest clutter struggles in this room? (Toys, clothing, paperwork, garbage, etc.?) How is the layout of the room working for you? What would you like to change?

Assignment:

1. **Remove and put away any items that belong in other rooms**. If necessary, use a basket to collect items, then distribute them to their proper homes.

2. **Clear all flat surfaces**—tables, desks, consoles, shelves, etc. Collect all items (picture frames, candles, decorative knick knacks) in one area, such as the dining room table or kitchen counter. De-clutter remaining items.

   Keep only the items that:
   - Are currently useful
   - Are in good working order
   - You absolutely love and want to display

   Do not keep items that:
   - You don't use
   - You don't like
   - You feel obligated to keep because it was expensive
   - You feel obligated to keep because it was a gift
   - Are constantly in your way

3. **Remove any furniture that is no longer working for your space**, whether it is broken or damaged or simply not a good fit for the room. Either throw it away, donate it, or sell it on Craigslist or Facebook, then, if necessary, rearrange remaining furniture to make your layout more functional.

LIVING ROOM INSPIRATION

Living Room Inspiration
1. Sunny Mid Century (WestElm.com)
2. Simple Statement Living Room (RealSimple.com)
3. Elegant Living Room (HomeDIT.com)
4. Calm and Clean Living Room (RealSimple.com)
5. Bright Brownstone Living Room (WestElm.com)

Day 4 Checklist:

- ☐ Take a "before" photo
- ☐ Remove and put away any items that belong in other rooms.
- ☐ Clear all flat surfaces and gather items in one space to declutter.
  - *Keep only the items that:*
    - Are currently useful
    - Are in good working order
    - You absolutely love and want to display
  - *Do NOT keep items that:*
    - You don't use
    - You don't like
    - You feel obligated to keep because it was expensive
    - You feel obligated to keep because it was a gift
    - Are constantly in your way
- ☐ Remove any furniture that is no longer working for the space.
- ☐ Rearrange remaining furniture to make layout more functional.
- ☐ Dust, sweep, vacuum, and clean glass surfaces.
- ☐ Label any storage containers.
- ☐ Immediately sell or donate unwanted items.
- ☐ Take an "after" photo and share on Instagram, Facebook, Pinterest, or Twitter with the hashtag #LWSLClutterFree!

$\mathcal{D}ay\,5$: Books and Magazines

Even in the age of eBooks and the Internet we still have not outgrown books. There's something almost magical about turning pages and many writers and poets have waxed lovingly about the feel, texture and even scent of reading materials.

All of this book love can make it difficult to part with books. Our homes become libraries housing tomes of literature we fell in love with. Letting go of a book sometimes feels like saying goodbye to a friend.

And while letting go of books can present one problem, organizing all those well-loved books can sometimes be a challenge as well. Different shapes and sizes can be hard to store, plus they are heavy and take up a lot of room. Unfortunately, paper can yellow, fade, and attract dust mites and mildew. Storing endless paperbacks is not feasible or necessarily even healthy. As with all organizing, pare down to the things that are really important to you.

First ask yourself if you, or anyone in your house, will be reading the book again or will reference the book. If you can't commit to sitting down with the book for another go, it's time to pass it on. Libraries, schools, and churches will often take book donations. Also consider building a Little Free Library or another outside-the-box organization/donation method for books.

Magazines and other periodicals can also be clutter disasters. Digital subscriptions and services that offer access to several magazines (like Next Issue, for example) can really cut back on the clutter. For print magazines, make it a policy to read them once and then pass them on, or tear out the pages you like and keep them in a single binder.

Start a magazine exchange with a few girlfriends that have similar tastes or donate extras to a doctor's office or another business' waiting room area. (Mechanics and salons are often grateful to give customers reading material, just black out your subscription information first.) Unless you truly reference scholarly journals or instructional magazines, most things can be found online or at a local library and there is no reason to save periodicals beyond their date.

Objective: A collection of books and magazines that you enjoy reading, stored in a functional and organized space.

Assess the current situation: What is the current state of your books and magazines? Do you have too many? How are they currently stored and organized? What are your biggest clutter struggles when it comes to books and magazines? What would you like to change?

Assignment:

1. **Toss or recycle any magazines you no longer wish to read.** There is no point in holding on to magazines you have no intention of reading again. If you are holding on to a particular magazine because of one article or recipe, simply tear out the page and create a binder to store your saved articles. (You could also consider taking a picture of the page and storing it digitally!)

2. **Declutter books.** Gather all the books in the house and bring them to one central location to sort and declutter.

    Keep only the books that:
    - You or a member of your family plans to read or refer to again
    - Are in good shape
    - You absolutely love and want to display

    Do not keep books that:
    - You don't read
    - You don't like
    - You feel obligated to keep because it was expensive
    - You feel obligated to keep because it was a gift

3. **Donate unwanted books to a local library or thrift shop.** Many libraries welcome used books, if not to use in the library then to sell for additional fundraising. Most second-hand stores also accept books. Alternatively, you could try selling your used books on Amazon Marketplace (though I recommend getting rid of items as quickly as possible.

4. **Create a functional storage area for your remaining books and magazines**. Be sure to sort them in a way that makes sense and makes them easy to access, such as like books together. Label shelves or bins.

BOOKS & MAGAZINE INSPIRATION

www.LivingWellSpendingLess.com

Photo Credit: West Elm, Real Simple
BHG, Home Depot

Books & Magazine Inspiration
1. Light & Lovely Library (WestElm.com)
2. Clutter Free Library (RealSimple.com)
3. Modern Magazine Storage (WestElm.com)
4. Color Scheme Storage (BHG.com)
5. Bench Book Cubbies (HomeDepot.com)

Day 5 Checklist:

☐ Take a "before" photo
☐ Toss or recycle any magazines you no longer want to read.
☐ Bring all books to one central location to sort.
  - **Keep only the books that:**
    - You or a family member plan to read or reference again
    - Are in good shape
    - You absolutely love and want to display
  - **Do NOT keep books that:**
    - You don't read
    - You don't like
    - You feel obligated to keep because it was expensive
    - You feel obligated to keep because it was a gift
☐ Organize magazines by title, month, and year
☐ Organize books by subject matter
☐ Create a functional storage area for books and magazines
☐ Dust, sweep, vacuum, and clean glass surfaces in book/magazine area.
☐ Label shelves or storage containers if necessary.
☐ Immediately donate unwanted books to a local library or thrift shop, or consider selling them on Amazon Marketplace.
☐ Take an "after" photo and share on Instagram, Facebook, Pinterest, or Twitter with the hashtag #LWSLClutterFree!

$\mathcal{D}ay$ 6: DVDs and Video Games

Video games, DVDs and other media are largely a modern phenomenon, but one that can easily get out of control. While watching whatever we want, whenever we want, can be deeply satisfying and entertaining, it can also be a major source of clutter and mess. Video game consoles become a tangle of cords, controllers and cases, and nothing is more frustrating than sitting down to watch a favorite movie only to find that it is not in the proper case.

Fear not! Taking just a little time to organize video games, DVDs and entertainment media can be simple and it will really pay off. With Netflix, HBO GO, Hulu and Amazon, almost anything can be instantly streamed and watched, which means that hopefully within a few years, DVD and video clutter will be a thing of the past!

For those films (particularly children's movies) that get watched (or games that get played) over and over, purchase only the items you can fit in an allotted space. Store them in a labeled container or organizer and reassess frequently. Sell, donate or trade-in used films and games and never keep something that is scratched, damaged or that you no longer love.

A word about VHS: Film does not age well and many VHS tapes will naturally "erase" or become damaged and unreadable over time. If you are still holding on to home movies on VHS, it is important to have them digitally archived so you do not lose these treasured memories. Look for a local service to copy these treasures onto DVD, which you can then back up in your digital archives.

Objective: A collection of DVDs and video games that you actually watch or play, stored in a functional and organized space.

Assess the current situation: What is the current state of your DVDs and video games? Do you have too many? Are there some you never watch? Do you have empty cases or discs with no cases? How are they currently stored and organized? What are your biggest clutter struggles when it comes to DVDs and video games? What would you like to change?

Assignment:

1. **Declutter**. Gather all DVDs and video games throughout the house and bring to one central location to sort and declutter.

   Keep only the DVDs or video games that:
   - You or a member of your family plans to watch or play again
   - Are in good shape (i.e. not scratched or damaged)

   Do not keep DVDs or video games that:
   - You don't plan to watch or play again
   - You don't like
   - You feel obligated to keep because it was expensive
   - You feel obligated to keep because it was a gift

2. **Donate unwanted DVDs and video games.** Most local libraries or thrift shops will gladly accept them; you may also consider selling any games or DVDs that may be valuable.

3. **Create a functional storage area for your remaining DVDs and video games.** Be sure to sort them in a way that makes sense and makes them easy to access, and LABEL EVERYTHING so that everyone in your family knows where things go!

4. **Have any old home movies transferred to digital format.** VHS tape will break down over time, so preserve those memories by having them transferred to DVD or digital format as soon as possible.

www.LivingWellSpendingLess.com

Photo Credits: BHG, West Elm, Ikea, Real Simple

DVD & Video Inspiration
1. Simpler Media Storage (BHG.com)
2. Sophisticated Storage (WestElm.com)
3. A Place For Everything Living Room (BHG.com)
4. Elegant & Inexpensive Storage Solutions (Ikea.com)
5. Pretty & Practical (RealSimple.com)

Day 6 Checklist:

- ☐ Take a "before" photo
- ☐ Bring all DVDs and video games to one central location to sort.
  - • *Keep only the DVDs or video games that:*
    - ▪ You or a family member plan to watch or play again
    - ▪ Are in good shape
  - • *Do NOT keep DVDs or video games that:*
    - ▪ You don't plan to watch or play again
    - ▪ You don't like
    - ▪ You feel obligated to keep because it was expensive
    - ▪ You feel obligated to keep because it was a gift
- ☐ Organize DVDs by genre
- ☐ Organize video games by genre
- ☐ Create a functional storage area for DVDs, video games, and related equipment.
- ☐ Dust, sweep, vacuum, and clean glass surfaces in DVD/video game storage areas.
- ☐ Label shelves or storage containers if necessary.
- ☐ Immediately donate unwanted DVDs and video games to a local library or thrift shop, or consider selling them on Amazon Marketplace, Craigslist, or Facebook.
- ☐ Take an "after" photo and share on Instagram, Facebook, Pinterest, or Twitter with the hashtag #LWSLClutterFree!

Day 7: Toys

Anyone who has read my now-infamous post about why I took my kids' toys away (and why they won't get them back) probably already knows that I am not a big fan of toys, especially not in excessive quantities. (Those who haven't read it can find it at www.LivingWellSpendingLess.com/toys.)

The truth is that no child needs a whole room full of toys, regardless of whether those toys happen to be expensive name-brand items or fantastic hand-me-down bargains snagged at a neighbor's yard sale.

Regardless of how much was spent, the result is the same. Kids are overwhelmed by their choices so they take everything out and play with nothing. Do yourself and your family a favor by drastically limiting the number of toys your children own, as well as the number of toys they have access to at any given time, and I promise your life will suddenly become a whole lot easier.

Objective: A small but purposeful collection of toys and games that your children actually play with, stored in a functional and organized space.

Assess the current situation: What is the current state of your children's toys? Do they have too many? Are there some toys they never play with? How are they currently stored and organized? What are your biggest clutter struggles when it comes to your kids' toys? What would you like to change?

Assignment:

1. **Bring all toys to one central location to sort.** Depending on your kids' ages and personalities, you may want to involve them in this process.

   ### Keep only toys or games that:
   - Your children play with regularly
   - Are in good condition
   - Are "special" in some way
   - Encourage imaginative and creative play

   ### Do not keep toys or games that:
   - Your children don't play with
   - Are broken, damaged, or missing key pieces
   - You feel obligated to keep because they were expensive
   - You feel obligated to keep because they were a gift
   - Drive you crazy
   - Cause fights among your children
   - Have a million tiny pieces that constantly end up on the floor

2. **Donate unwanted toys and games.** Consider giving them to a local thrift shop, church nursery, or daycare facility, or try selling any larger items that may be valuable on Craigslist or Facebook.

3. **Create a functional storage area for your remaining toys and games**. Be sure to sort them in a way that makes sense and makes them easy to access, and LABEL EVERYTHING! Consider separating the toys into 2-4 different bundles, and then rotate your kids' access to the different bundles on a weekly or monthly basis. This keeps the quantity of toys out at one time to a minimum and makes all the toys more interesting and exciting for your kids.

TOY INSPIRATION

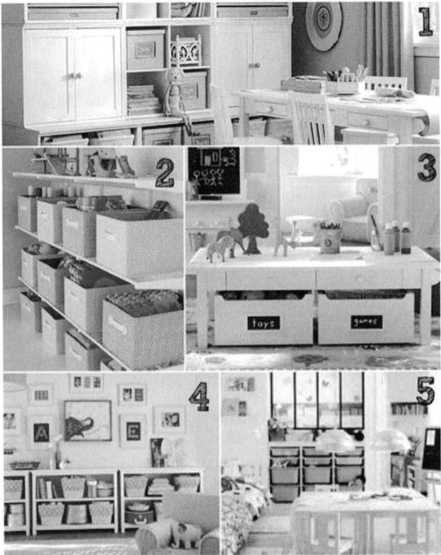

www.LivingWellSpendingLess.com

Photo Credit: Pottery Barn Kids,
Container Store, Ikea,

Toy Inspiration
1. Princess Perfection Playroom (PotteryBarnKids.com)
2. Tackle The Toy Mess (ContainerStore.com)
3. Tuck Away Table (PotteryBarnKids.com)
4. Shade of Grey Storage (PotteryBarnKids.com)
5. Plenty Of Room For Play (Ikea.com)

Day 7 Checklist:

☐ Take a "before" photo
☐ Bring all toys to one central location to sort.
- *Keep only the toys that:*
  - Your children play with regularly
  - Are in good condition
  - Are genuinely "special" in some way
  - Encourage imaginative and creative play
- *Do NOT keep toys that:*
  - Your children don't really like or play with.
  - Are broken, damaged, or are missing key pieces.
  - You feel obligated to keep because they were expensive
  - You feel obligated to keep because they were a gift
  - Drive you crazy
  - Cause fights among your children
  - Have a million tiny pieces that constantly end up on the floor

☐ Sort and organize toys by type
☐ Create a functional storage area for remaining toys and games.
☐ Consider separating toys into 2-4 different bundles that can be rotated on a weekly or monthly basis.
☐ Dust, sweep, vacuum, and clean glass surfaces toy/play area.
☐ Label shelves or storage containers if necessary.
☐ Immediately donate unwanted toys to a local day-care, church nursery, or thrift shop, or consider selling them on Craigslist or Facebook.
☐ Take an "after" photo and share on Instagram, Facebook, Pinterest, or Twitter with the hashtag #LWSLClutterFree!

$\mathcal{D}ay\,8$: Junk Drawer

While maintaining a "junk" drawer might seem counterintuitive to a challenge that is intended to rid our lives of excess clutter, the reality is that this type of catchall space holds an important purpose in a well organized, clutter-free home. The fact is, not every single item we own can be easily categorized into a larger, more purposeful space. Sometimes we just need a place to hold on to the little things so we know where to find them when we need them. That said, it is also important to keep this space from becoming too, well, junky.

Objective: An organized an purposeful "junk drawer" that serves as a catchall for life's little necessities that otherwise might not have a home.

Assess the current situation: What is the current state of your junk drawer? Do you actually use the items that are found there? Do you currently throw things in at random, or do only certain things belong? Do you have more than one junk drawer? How many catchall drawers do you think are realistically necessary in your home? What are your biggest clutter struggles when it comes to your junk drawer? What would you like to change?

Assignment:

1. **Declutter.** If you have multiple junk drawers, only focus on one drawer at a time. Empty the drawer of all contents, then sort and purge:

   ### Keep only items that:
   - Are currently useful
   - Are in good condition and good working order
   - Don't have another home

   ### Do not items that:
   - Belong somewhere else
   - Are broken, damaged, or missing key pieces
   - You feel obligated to keep because they were expensive
   - You feel obligated to keep because they were a gift
   - Drive you crazy
   - You don't use
   - You don't need or want

2. **Get rid of unwanted items.** Donate them to a local thrift shop if appropriate, or consider selling any expensive items that may be valuable on Craigslist or Facebook.

3. **Create a functional storage space for your remaining junk drawer items.** Be sure to sort them in a way that makes sense and makes them easy to access. Use drawer dividers to create specific areas for each item, and LABEL EVERY-THING so that everyone in your family knows where each item belongs!

JUNK DRAWER INSPIRATION

Junk Drawer Inspiration
1. Tidy & Tucked Away (RealSimple.com)
2. Unclutter Your Drawers (LiveSimplyByAnnie.com)
3. Divide & Conquer (Umbrinco.com)
4. Tame Your Junk (BHG.com)
5. Everything Organized (ContainerStore.com)

Day 8 Checklist:

- ☐ Take a "before" photo
- ☐ Empty the contents of your junk drawer, then sort and purge.
  - • **Keep only the items that:**
    - ▪ Are currently useful
    - ▪ Are in good condition and good working order
    - ▪ Don't have another home
  - • **Do NOT keep items that:**
    - ▪ Belong somewhere else
    - ▪ Are broken, damaged, or are missing key pieces.
    - ▪ You feel obligated to keep because they were expensive
    - ▪ You feel obligated to keep because they were a gift
    - ▪ Drive you crazy
    - ▪ You don't use
    - ▪ You don't want
- ☐ Return items that belong elsewhere to their proper places
- ☐ Wipe drawer clean of dust, spills, and debris
- ☐ Create a functional storage area for remaining junk drawer items
  - • Sort items in a way that makes sense
  - • Use drawer dividers to keep things in place
- ☐ Label everything so everyone in your family knows what goes where.
- ☐ Immediately donate, toss, or sell unwanted items.
- ☐ Take an "after" photo and share on Instagram, Facebook, Pinterest, or Twitter with the hashtag #LWSLClutterFree!

$\mathcal{D}ay\,9$: **Dining Area**

Sharing meals together is one of the most important things you can do for your family. Believe it or not, family dinners are more important than play, reading stories, or any other family events in young children's vocabulary development. Furthermore, kids who eat more often with their parents are far more likely to earn all A's and B's in school, and far less likely to smoke, use drugs, become depressed, or develop eating disorders.[1]

I don't know about you, but for me those are some pretty compelling reasons to make sure that my family's dining area is ready for, well, *dining*. The problem in this space, of course, is that dining tables are useful for so many other things, such as homework, playing bills, doing puzzles or craft projects, or holding all the paper clutter or other items we're just not sure what to do with.

The key, then, to tackling this space, is to make sure that the table surface is kept clear but that there are nearby storage solutions for any other uses that the table may serve.

Objective: An open, comfortable, and inviting dining space for guests and family to gather, connect, relax, and eat together.

Assess the current situation: How is this room used right now? List all the purposes of this room. What are the biggest clutter strug-

---

1   http://dinnertrade.com/568/interesting-statistics-on-family-dinners

gles in this room? (Toys, clothing, paperwork, garbage, etc.?) How is the layout of the room working for you? What would you like to change?

Assignment:

1. **Remove and put away any items that belong in other rooms.** If necessary, use a basket to collect items, then distribute them to their proper homes.

2. **Clear all flat surfaces**—dining table, shelves, buffets. Collect all items (picture frames, candles, decorative knick knacks) in one area, such as the dining room table or kitchen counter. De-clutter remaining items.

   ### Keep only the items that:
   - Are currently useful
   - Are in good working order
   - You absolutely love and want to display

   ### Do not keep items that:
   - You don't use
   - You don't like
   - You feel obligated to keep because it was expensive
   - You feel obligated to keep because it was a gift
   - Are constantly in your way

3. **Remove any furniture that is no longer working for your space**, whether it is broken or damaged or simply not a good fit for the room. Either throw it away, donate it, or sell it on Craigslist or Facebook; then, if necessary, rearrange remaining furniture to make your layout more functional.

4. **Create dedicated storage areas in this space that coincide with the way the space is used.** Do you pay bills and sort paperwork at the table? Consider adding a pretty file cabinet that can hold all your necessary items for when you need them. Is this where your family does homework or crafts? Determine what items you need and create simple storage solutions that work.

DINING AREA INSPIRATION

www.LivingWellSpendingLess.com

Photo Credit: BHG, Ikea, Real Simple
ArchitectureArtDesigns.com

Dining Area Inspiration
1. Sophisticated Storage For Entertaining (BHG.com)
2. Ideas That Bring Everyone To The Table (Ikea.com)
3. Classic Comfort Cube Storage (ArchitectureArtDesigns.com)
4. Storage That Satisfies Your Cravings (Ikea.com)
5. Mix & Match Storage Style (RealSimple.com)

Day 9 Checklist:

☐ Take a "before" photo
☐ Remove and put away any items that belong in other rooms.
☐ Clear all flat surfaces and gather items in one space to declutter.
- **Keep only the items that:**
  - Are currently useful
  - Are in good working order
  - You absolutely love and want to display
- **Do NOT keep items that:**
  - You don't use
  - You don't like
  - You feel obligated to keep because it was expensive
  - You feel obligated to keep because it was a gift
  - Are constantly in your way
☐ Remove any furniture that is no longer working for the space.
☐ Rearrange remaining furniture to make layout more functional.
☐ Create dedicated storage space for any specific functions of this room, such as paying bills, sewing, or crafting.
☐ Dust, sweep, vacuum, and clean glass surfaces.
☐ Label any storage containers.
☐ Immediately sell or donate unwanted items.
☐ Take an "after" photo and share on Instagram, Facebook, Pinterest, or Twitter with the hashtag #LWSLClutterFree!

$\mathcal{D}ay$ 10: Kitchen Counters

Like the dining table, the ample flat surface area provided by kitchen counters is often a catch-all for, well, everything—mail, an endless stream of school papers, groceries, appliances, dishes that need to be put away, fruit bowls, the butter dish, salt and pepper shakers, loaves of bread, recycling......you name it. If it comes in the kitchen, it will most likely end up on the counter.

The problem with this is that cluttered counters do not a happy kitchen make! It is difficult and frustrating to try to cook and work on counters full of things that don't belong.

The trick to tackling this easily cluttered space will be to establish a clear and vigilant no-clutter policy by removing everything but the barest essentials, and then creating a collection zone for the items that find their way in so that they can be quickly removed.

Objective: Clear and functional kitchen counters that make cooking and working in the kitchen a pleasure instead of a chore.

Assess the current situation: How are your counters used right now? What are your biggest clutter struggles on the counters? What would you like to change?

Assignment:

1. **Remove and put away any items that belong in other rooms**. If necessary, use a basket to collect items, then distribute them to their proper homes.

2. **Clear and de-clutter counters**. Remove all items that are not absolutely critical, using the following criteria.

   Keep only the appliances or other items that:
   - You use more than three times a week
   - Are in good working order

   Do not keep items that:
   - You don't use
   - You don't like
   - You feel obligated to keep because they were expensive
   - You feel obligated to keep because they were a gift
   - Are constantly in your way

3. **Create new storage space**. You will need to create additional storage options for any appliances or other counter items that you still want to keep but don't use very often.

4. **Toss unwanted items, or donate them to a local thrift shop if appropriate**. Consider selling any expensive items that may be valuable on Craigslist or Facebook.

KITCHEN COUNTER INSPIRATION

www.LivingWellSpendingLess.com

Photo Credit: Ikea, BHG, HGTV, Real Simple

Kitchen Counter Inspiration
1. A Kitchen Catered to You (Ikea.com)
2. Dish Drawer For Snappy Table Setting (BHG.com)
3. Ditch the Bulky Boxes & Save Space At the Same Time (HGTV.com)
4. Clutter Free Countertops (RealSimple.com)
5. Form & Function- Kitchen Island & Storage Area (Ikea.com)

Day 10 Checklist:

- ☐ Take a "before" photo
- ☐ Remove and put away any items that belong in other rooms.
- ☐ Clear and declutter counters.
  - • **Keep only the appliances or other items that:**
    - ▪ You use more than 3 times per week
    - ▪ Are in good working order
    - ▪ You absolutely love and want to display
  - • **Do NOT keep items that:**
    - ▪ You don't use
    - ▪ You don't like
    - ▪ You feel obligated to keep because it was expensive
    - ▪ You feel obligated to keep because it was a gift
    - ▪ Are constantly in your way
- ☐ Create new storage options for appliances you want to keep but don't use very often.
- ☐ Rearrange remaining appliances to make layout more functional.
- ☐ Wipe down counters.
- ☐ Label any storage containers.
- ☐ Immediately sell, toss, or donate unwanted items.
- ☐ Take an "after" photo and share on Instagram, Facebook, Pinterest, or Twitter with the hashtag #LWSLClutterFree!

$\mathcal{D}$ay 11: Kitchen Cupboards and Drawers

With your newly-cleared counter surfaces to inspire you, it is time to dig a little deeper, into those sometimes-scary-but-usually-hidden areas behind closed doors Yes, it is time to tackle the kitchen cupboards (and drawers.)

How ironic that the exact feature that makes them so useful—closed doors—is the feature that also makes them so prone to clutter and to collecting far more kitchen items than we can realistically use? The key to permanently ridding this zone of clutter will be a combination of refusing to store the unessential and vigilantly labeling *everything*.

Objective: Organized and functional kitchen cupboards and drawers that contain only the essentials and make necessary items easy to find.

Assess the current situation: How are your cupboards being used right now? What are your biggest clutter struggles in your kitchen cupboards? What would you like to change?

Assignment:

1. **Remove and put away any items that belong in other rooms.** If necessary, use a basket to collect items, then distribute them to their proper homes.

2. **Clear and declutter.** Working one drawer or cabinet at a time, clear and declutter each individual space.

   For non-food cabinets/drawers:

   Keep only the tools, dishes, or kitchen items that:
   - You use regularly
   - Are in good working order
   - Are in good condition

   Do not keep items that:
   - You don't use
   - You don't like
   - You feel obligated to keep because they were expensive
   - You feel obligated to keep because they were a gift
   - Are constantly in your way

   For baking and seasoning cabinets/drawers:

   Keep only the baking and seasoning items that:
   - You use regularly

   Do not keep items that:
   - Are no longer fresh
   - You don't like

3. **Sort items by type and use.** Put like items together in a way that makes sense and creates the most functional use, such as baking supplies, pots and pans, cooking essentials, etc.

4. **Return items to cabinets or drawers in an organized fashion**, creating functional storage using containers or bins wherever necessary for smaller or perishable items.

5. **Label everything!** The more clearly a designated home for an item is labeled, the more likely it that it will be returned to its proper spot.

6. **Toss unwanted items, or donate them to a local thrift shop if appropriate.** Consider selling any expensive items that may be valuable on Craigslist or Facebook.

KITCHEN CUPBOARD INSPIRATION

www.LivingWellSpendingLess.com

Photo Credit: Real Simple, Ikea, BHG

Kitchen Cupboard Inspiration
1. Dishes on Display (RealSimple.com)
2. Smart Shelving (Ikea.com)
3. Kitchen Cabinets That Store More (BHG.com)
4. Categorize Foods (replace this image maybe) (RealSimple.com)
5. Basket Case (BHG.com)

Day 11 Checklist:

☐ Take a "before" photo

☐ Remove and put away any items that belong in other rooms.

☐ Working one space at a time, clear and declutter cupboards and drawers.

- ***For non-food items, keep only the kitchen tools or dishes that:***
  - You use regularly
  - Are in good working order or good condition
- ***For perishable items, keep only the items that:***
  - You use regularly
- ***Do NOT keep items that:***
  - You don't use
  - You don't like
  - You feel obligated to keep because it was expensive
  - You feel obligated to keep because it was a gift
  - Are constantly in your way
  - Are no longer fresh

☐ Sort items by type and use.

☐ Wipe down cabinets or drawers.

☐ Return items to appropriate cabinet or drawer

☐ Create functional storage using containers or bins

☐ Label everything

☐ Immediately sell, toss, or donate unwanted items.

☐ Take an "after" photo and share on Instagram, Facebook, Pinterest, or Twitter with the hashtag #LWSLClutterFree!

Day 12: Pantry

Now that you've tackled your cupboards, the next logical step is to declutter your food pantry. A well-stocked pantry is saves time by allowing you to keep essentials on hand, thus cutting back on trips to the store. An organized pantry also helps you save money by eliminating the need to eat out because there is nothing to eat.

Pay attention to staples that your family uses—pastas, cereals, low-sodium canned vegetables and fruit, beans and tomatoes, dried fruit, rice, grains, nut butters and baking ingredients. When you see these items on sale, stocking up on a few of each item can ensure you always have a go-to solution to feed your family.

By the same logic, pantries should be easily accessible, just like at the store: labels should be face-out and ingredients should be rotated regularly. Everything should be stored in airtight containers, clearly labeled and easy to access. It is important to remember that the pantry should NOT become a dumping ground for expired, strange or never-used ingredients. While some storage of lesser-used appliances, paper towels, and other items might be necessary, the primary purpose of a pantry is to store food.

Objective: A convenient and easily accessible pantry stocked with only staple, regularly used ingredients and basics for you and your family.

Assess the current situation: How much pantry space to you have? Are the items in your pantry old, expired or rarely used? What are the main staples your family uses during a typical week? Similar to your cupboards, what items are essential, and what items can be donated or thrown out? Are the shelves and storage containers appropriate or do you need other storage solutions?

Assignment:

1. **Remove and put away any items that belong in other rooms.** If necessary, use a basket to collect items, then distribute them to their proper homes.

2. **Empty pantry of all contents to sort.** Discard any open or expired items; rarely used ingredients that are unopened should be donated to your local food pantry.

   Keep only the pantry staples that:
   - Your family eats during a typical four-week period
   - Is not expired and unopened

   Do not keep items that:
   - You don't use
   - You don't like
   - Were specifically purchased for a one-time use or occasion
   - Have been opened (currently open items should be stored in the cupboard, rather than the pantry)
   - Are beyond their expiration date

3. **Return items to pantry in an organized fashion.** Pair like-items together and turn labels forward so they can be easily read. Place items with expiration dates far in the future at the back. Pasta and dry ingredients can be repackaged into dry, airtight storage containers or jars and labeled with expiration dates. (Tip: Freezing rice and pasta for 24 hours then storing in airtight containers can help prevent weevils!)

4. **Store bulky items.** Place paper towels, bulk food items, and rarely used appliances on the top or bottom shelves to keep ingredients at eye-level. Prioritize and keep only what you will use and what you can reasonably organize into the space.

5. **Ensure all items are accessible.** Consider storage solutions like stackable containers for dry ingredients.

6. **Toss unwanted items, or donate them to a local thrift shop if appropriate.** Consider selling any expensive items that may be valuable on Craigslist or Facebook.

PANTRY INSPIRATION

www.LivingWellSpendingLess.com

Photo Credit: Container Store, BHG, HGTV, Real Simple

Pantry Inspiration
1. Pretty Bakers Pantry (ContainersStore.com)
2. Pull Out Pantry (BHG.com)
3. Stash Items Over The Door (RealSimple.com)
4. Stay Well Stocked (HGTV.com)
5. Easy Finds (BHG.com)

Day 12 Checklist:

- ☐ Take a "before" photo
- ☐ Remove and put away any items that belong in other rooms.
- ☐ Empty pantry of all contents to sort.
  - • *Keep only the items that:*
    - ▪ Your family eats regularly
    - ▪ Is not expired
    - ▪ Are unopened
  - • *Do NOT keep items that:*
    - ▪ You don't use
    - ▪ You don't like
    - ▪ Were specifically purchased for a one-time use that has passed.
    - ▪ Have been opened (store in an "open items" cupboard instead
    - ▪ Are past their expiration date.
- ☐ Sort items by type and use.
- ☐ Wipe down pantry shelves
- ☐ Return items to pantry in an organized fashion.
- ☐ Create functional storage for dry goods using containers or bins
- ☐ Label everything
- ☐ Immediately sell, toss, or donate unwanted items.
- ☐ Take an "after" photo and share on Instagram, Facebook, Pinterest, or Twitter with the hashtag #LWSLClutterFree!

Day 13: Master Bedroom

Is your bedroom a sanctuary? If not, it should be. Most sleep experts recommend that your bedroom should be primarily for sleeping and relaxing. The room should be cool, calming and inviting. It should also be free of dust and clutter, particularly for allergy sufferers.

The sad truth is that in today's busy world, our beds often become places where we work, hang out with children and pets, eat, watch television, store things under, and do everything BUT sleep. However, proper sleep has been linked to weight loss, increased productivity, concentration and happiness, and general well-being. Ensuring your bedroom is a place where you and your partner can connect, relax and find solace and peace from the outside world is vital.

Whenever possible, bedrooms should have minimal décor and soothing colors. Bedding should be clean, dust-free and changed weekly. Pillows and mattresses are home to dust mites and should be encased in allergen-protective covers. Pillows should be washed monthly and replaced regularly (every 6-12 months is recommended.) Food (and yes, even pets) should be kept out of the bedroom. Under-bed storage should be minimal (if at all) and your bedroom should be free of electronics, piles of books and work, or anything that makes you feel uneasy.

Studies show that the ideal temperature for sleeping is 65 degrees. A fan can help ensure your bedroom stays cool as well as create white noise. Use caution with electronics in the bedroom—even the light created by an alarm clock or bedside phone can cause sleep disturbances. A small bedside table should hold a reading item, a water bottle, tissues, and little else. Lamps or soft lighting are preferred, as they help relax and prepare your body for sleep. Your bedroom should be a peaceful comforting place where you can rest soundly and awake refreshed and ready to face the day.

Objective: A relaxing bedroom sanctuary free of clutter that promotes and encourages good sleep practices.

Assess the current situation: What items do you truly need for sleep? What items can be removed from the bedroom and stored elsewhere? What do you store under your bed? What items are on your nightstand? What are your electronic, fan and lighting situations in the bedroom and how can these be improved?

Assignment:

1. **Remove and put away any items that belong in other rooms.** If necessary, use a basket to collect items, then distribute them to their proper homes. Be sure to especially focus on items that distract from sleeping.

2. **Sort and declutter.** Clear all flat surfaces and gather items in one place to sort and declutter.

   Keep only items that:
   - Pertain to sleep and bedtime
   - Are calming, soothing and relaxing
   - Are currently useful
   - Are in good working order
   - You absolutely love and want to display

   Do not keep items that:
   - Should be stored elsewhere
   - Interfere with your sleep
   - Cause you anxiety or reduce your concentration
   - You don't use
   - You don't like
   - You feel obligated to keep because it was expensive
   - You feel obligated to keep because it was a gift
   - Are constantly in your way

3. **Change bedding.** Ensure that comforters, pillows and blankets are washed and clean. Replace if necessary.

4. **Remove items that are stored under the bed.** Under-the-bed storage can add to an overall feeling of clutter in the

room. This area also tends to collect a lot of excess dust which is detrimental to healthy sleep.

5. **Remove any furniture that is no longer working for your space**, whether it is broken or damaged or simply not a good fit for the room. Either throw it away, donate it, or sell it on Craigslist or Facebook; then, if necessary, rearrange remaining furniture to make your layout more functional.

6. **Toss unwanted items, or donate them to a local thrift shop if appropriate.** Consider selling any expensive items that may be valuable on Craigslist or Facebook.

MASTER BEDROOM INSPIRATION

www.LivingWellSpendingLess.com

Photo Credit: Real Simple, Archi Magz, West Elm, Good House Keeping, Home Designer Ideas

Master Bedroom Inspiration
1. Traditional Elegance Work Space (RealSimple.com)
2. Contemporary Design with Practical Storage (ArchiMagz.com)
3. Simple Storage Solution (GoodHouseKeeping.com)
4. Mid Century Modern (WestElm.com)
5. Sweet Dreams Bed With Storage (HomeDesignerIdeas.com)

Day 13 Checklist:

- ☐ Take a "before" photo
- ☐ Remove and put away any items that belong in other rooms.
- ☐ Clear all flat surfaces and gather items in one space to declutter.
  - • ***Keep only the items that:***
    - ▪ Pertain to sleep and bedtime
    - ▪ Are calming, soothing and relaxing
    - ▪ Are currently useful
    - ▪ Are in good working order
    - ▪ You absolutely love and want to display
  - • ***Do NOT keep items that:***
    - ▪ Should be stored elsewhere
    - ▪ Interfere with your sleep
    - ▪ Cause you anxiety or reduce your concentration
    - ▪ You don't use
    - ▪ You don't like
    - ▪ You feel obligated to keep because it was expensive
    - ▪ You feel obligated to keep because it was a gift
    - ▪ Are constantly in your way
- ☐ Change bedding and replace if necessary.
- ☐ Remove any furniture that is no longer working for the space.
- ☐ Rearrange remaining furniture to make layout more functional.
- ☐ Make subtle changes in lighting, sound, and décor to help create a more relaxing space.

☐ Dust, sweep, vacuum, and clean glass surfaces.

☐ Label any storage containers.

☐ Immediately sell or donate unwanted items.

☐ Take an "after" photo and share on Instagram, Facebook, Pinterest, or Twitter with the hashtag #LWSLClutterFree!

$\mathcal{D}ay$ 14: Master Closet and Drawers

Closets vary greatly in shapes, sizes and storage solutions. Just like variations in each person's own personal style, each closet is completely different too. Perhaps you share a closet with your spouse. Perhaps you are lucky enough to have a walk-in closet. Perhaps you live in an apartment where an out-of-the-box wardrobe is your only solution to clothing storage.

No matter the space, having a closet that is easily accessible, clean, organized and beautiful is key; your entire persona, your style and your sense of self will benefit from having a great closet.

Imagine quickly finding items every morning and always having great outfits that are in-style, clean, in good repair and fit properly—right at your fingertips! How much easier would that be, rather than frantically searching for a matching pair of socks, dealing with a broken heel, realizing there is a snag in your sweater, or discovering a fallen pant hem?

Not only does proper closet storage make it easier to feel and look great, but it truly prolongs the life of your clothing because closet organization means your clothing is not stretched, smashed and wrinkled, or tossed on the floor. You will get more wear out of your outfits and they will last longer when they are stored neatly with plenty of space.

Objective: An organized master closet space that houses your current wardrobe in a clean, easily accessible manner.

Assess the current situation: What items need repair, are soiled, stained, snagged or show signs of wear? How much closet space do you have, realistically? What accessories need to be stored in your closet and do you have the proper containers to do so? Do you love everything in your closet? Does your clothing flatter you and is it currently in style?

Assignment:

1. **Remove and put away any items that belong in other rooms.** If necessary, use a basket to collect items, then distribute them to their proper homes.

2. **Assess each item of clothing in your closet and drawers—** does it fit? Is it flattering? Is it in good condition? Have you worn it in the last six months? This may require that you try on items, one at a time. Sort your clothing into three piles— keep, donate and maybe.

   ### *Keep only items that:*
   - Fit, flatter and make you feel great
   - Are in good to excellent condition
   - Are part of an outfit or "go" with other items you own
   - Are classic cuts, stylish and well-made

   ### *Do not keep items that:*
   - You are holding onto out of regret or guilt, or to those items you're hoping to fit into again "someday"
   - Are soiled, stained or cannot be quickly pressed or repaired
   - You don't feel great and confident wearing
   - Were trendy at the time, but are now painfully out of style
   - You have not worn within the last six months (or the last year for special occasion items)

3. **Re-assess the maybe pile.** Discard anything that cannot be repaired or cleaned within one week. Let go of anything you don't love or that doesn't fit.

4. **Assess shoes.** Polish if needed and wipe bottoms with a damp cloth. Store all shoes in a shoe rack or container.

   Keep only items that:
   - Fit
   - You can wear for an entire day or walk in for a half an hour
   - Do not require more than a polish or a quick fix (or those you will repair within one week)

   Do not keep items that:
   - Are uncomfortable
   - Are out of style
   - Will not fit in your allotted space

5. **Assess folded items and accessories.** Hang scarves and ties on proper hangers, discard or donate any item you have not worn or used in six months. Store handbags, empty and clean, stuffed with tissue paper and housed in stackable boxes.

6. **Hang clothing by type, length and color.** Face hangers the same direction, leaving at least half an inch between each item. Use proper hangers for slacks and skirts. Keep only items that will fit in your allotted space.

7. **Keep it organized.** Going forward, start on one side of your closet and wear a different item each day, taking a quick snapshot of yourself each morning. When you get to an item that you don't want to wear, or discover upon wearing that it doesn't fit, flatter or needs to be fixed, discard or donate it rather than putting it back in the closet.

MASTER CLOSET INSPIRATION

www.LivingWellSpendingLess.com

Master Closet Inspiration
1. Custom Closet Organization (BHG.com)
2. Customizable Closet Systems (ContainerStore.com)
3. Dream Walk In (EasyClosets.com)
4. Modern Masculine (Ikea.com)
5. Create Your Ideal Closet (MarthaStewart.com)

Day 14 Checklist:

- ☐ Take a "before" photo
- ☐ Remove and put away any items that belong in other rooms.
- ☐ Assess each item of clothing in your closet and drawers—does it fit? Is it flattering? Is it in good condition? Have you worn it in the last six months? This may require that you try on items, one at a time. Sort your clothing into three piles—keep, donate and maybe.
  - *Keep only items that:*
    - Fit, flatter and make you feel great
    - Are in good to excellent condition
    - Are part of an outfit or "go" with other items you own
    - Are classic cuts, stylish and well-made
  - *Do not keep items that:*
    - You are holding onto out of regret or guilt
    - Are soiled, stained or cannot be quickly pressed or repaired
    - You don't feel great and confident wearing
    - Were trendy at the time, but are now painfully out of style
    - You have not worn within the last six months
- ☐ Assess folded items using the same criteria.
- ☐ Create functional storage for accessories
- ☐ Return clothing to closet and drawers, hanging clothing by type, length and color.
- ☐ Dust, sweep, vacuum, and clean glass surfaces.
- ☐ Label any storage containers.
- ☐ Immediately sell or donate unwanted items.
- ☐ Take an "after" photo and share on Instagram, Facebook, Pinterest, or Twitter with the hashtag #LWSLClutterFree!

$\mathcal{D}ay$ 15: Master Bathroom

An organized master bathroom can diminish stress and help you in a variety of ways. From more efficient mornings to better hygiene, skin care and general health, having an organized master bathroom is key. Just like a command center for your home, your master bathroom is a command center for your body and beauty.

Second to the kitchen, the master bathroom is probably one of the biggest areas of clutter accumulation, and one of the most challenging areas to keep clean. Beauty and bath products can pile up in drawers—and hair, hairspray, moisture and mildew add to the mix, making it a perfect storm of gross and grime (and that's not even counting the toilet).

Yet, the master bath is a place that we clean the dirt of the world off our bodies, so it should become a sanctuary where we can literally put on our best face to the world. Organization and cleanliness is mandatory in this area of your home.

Objective: A clean, organized "body command center."

Assess the current situation: What products do you use daily? Weekly? Are you utilizing storage space efficiently? Where does dirt, grime and mildew hide in the bathroom and how can you prevent it?

Assignment:

1. **Remove and put away any items that belong in other rooms.** If necessary, use a basket to collect items, then distribute them to their proper homes.

2. **Sort and Declutter.** Remove all items from drawers, under-sink cabinets, vanity and other areas. Discard anything that has not been used within the last three months. Check all expiration dates and discard anything that is over six months old. (Lotion can separate, and sunscreen and other products lose effectiveness and can even go rancid.)

    Keep only items that:
    - You use regularly
    - You like and work for you
    - Are in good repair

    Do not keep items that:
    - Are expired, leaking or in broken containers
    - You no longer use or didn't fit your needs
    - Are over six months old
    - Are sensitive to heat or moisture (like medications)
    - Are decorative but difficult to keep clean

3. **Clean.** Thoroughly wipe down all surfaces, insides of drawers and cabinets, and shower surfaces. Shower organizers can be scrubbed or run through your dishwasher.

4. **Organize.** Place "like" items together—for example: hair products and accessories, shower products, under-sink storage items.

5. **Beautify.** If you like, line drawers with pretty paper or drawer liners.

6. **Create functional storage areas in your drawers and cabinets.** Use lidded clear plastic containers to house smaller items in drawers. Organize larger bottles in plastic crates with drainage for storage under the sink. Separate them into large plastic bags and label with markers. Toilet paper, feminine hygiene items and other products can be stored under the sink.

7. **Organize shower and bath products into a drainable caddy**—keep one of each type of product (one shampoo, one conditioner, etc.). Hang a squeegee in your shower and spray for quick cleaning after each use. Discard any sponges, loofahs, or other items that are more than one month old (they are a prime area for bacteria growth) and run synthetic scrubbies through the wash on a weekly basis to disinfect.

Master Bath Inspiration

www.LivingWellSpendingLess.com

Photo Credit: Ikea, HGTV, Martha Stewart
Real Simple, Good House Keeping

Master Bath Inspiration
1. Storage Packed Master Bath (Ikea.com)
2. Cabinets Galore (HGTV.com)
3. Clever Bathroom Storage (MarthaStewart.com)
4. Tame Your Hair Dryer (RealSimple.com)
5. Casual Cabinet (GoodHouseKeeping.com)

Day 15 Checklist:

- ☐ Take a "before" photo
- ☐ Remove and put away any items that belong in other rooms.
- ☐ Remove all items from drawers, under-sink cabinets, vanity and other areas to sort and declutter.
  - • *Keep only items that:*
    - ▪ You use regularly
    - ▪ You like and work for you
    - ▪ Are in good repair
  - • *Do not keep items that:*
    - ▪ Are expired, leaking or in broken containers
    - ▪ You no longer use or didn't fit your needs
    - ▪ Are over six months old
    - ▪ Are sensitive to heat or moisture (like medications)
    - ▪ Are decorative but difficult to keep clean
- ☐ Thoroughly wipe down all surfaces, insides of drawers and cabinets, and shower surfaces.
- ☐ Create functional storage areas in your drawers and cabinets. Use lidded clear plastic containers to house smaller items in drawers. Organize larger bottles in plastic crates with drainage for storage under the sink. Separate them into large plastic bags and label with markers. Toilet paper, feminine hygiene items and other products can be stored under the sink.
- ☐ Organize shower and bath products into a drainable caddy
- ☐ Hang a squeegee in your shower and spray for quick cleaning after each use.

- ☐ Dust, sweep, vacuum, and clean glass surfaces.
- ☐ Label any storage containers.
- ☐ Immediately sell or donate unwanted items.
- ☐ Take an "after" photo and share on Instagram, Facebook, Pinterest, or Twitter with the hashtag #LWSLClutterFree!

Day 16: Medicine Cabinet

The term medicine cabinet, at least in the bathroom, is a misnomer. A bathroom is actually one of the worst places to store medication, as heat and moisture can be an enemy to pills, vitamins, and over-the-counter products. Instead, choose a cabinet in another area of your home: preferably a dry, temperature-controlled, kid-proof pantry shelf or separate cupboard.

As always, paring down the items to what you truly need helps. Always check expiration dates and never buy more than you will use in that time—even with a coupon.

Remove all expired pills and potions, but be careful about simply throwing these items away or flushing them down the toilet! Expired and unused medications and vitamins can contaminate the local water supply and poison the land. Most communities offer civic days where medicines can dropped off at a centralized repository. Many hospitals and pharmacies will also accept your expired medications. You can also try senior centers or water municipalities in your area. It might take a little online research and a couple phone calls, but it's definitely worth the extra legwork.

Place items you use daily, such as vitamins and prescriptions, toward the front of the cabinet for easy access. Rarely or occasionally used items should be placed toward the back. Be sure all labels are facing forward so you don't have to go digging next time your poor kid gets the flu. Consider using a tiered cabinet organizer or plastic bins to help keep all those bottles easier to access.

Overflow items and long-lasting items that you have stocked up on can be sorted into labeled bags and housed in stackable bins on the lower shelves and toward the back of your medicine cabinet.

Having a well-organized medicine cabinet can not only be a timesaver, but it's a money-saver too, as you can very quickly assess what you have on hand and the status of each item when you make your shopping lists.

Objective: An organized and easily accessible medicine cabinet.

Assess the current situation: What items are used most frequently? What items are used only once in a while? Is your medicine cabinet dry and free from moisture? Are you utilizing storage space efficiently?

Assignment:

1. **Remove and put away any items that belong in other rooms.** If necessary, use a basket to collect items, then distribute them to their proper homes.

2. **Sort and declutter.** Remove the items from your medicine cabinet and assess each one.

   Keep only items that:
   - Are used by your family, both regularly and on occasion
   - Are unexpired
   - Do the trick

   Do not keep items that:
   - Are expired, leaking or in broken containers
   - You no longer use or didn't fit your needs
   - Need to be replaced
   - Are over six months old

3. **Clean.** Wipe out the inside of your medicine cabinet and line the shelves with pretty paper.

4. **Return items to cabinet.** Organize like-items by shelf (daily vitamins, kids' medications, prescriptions, flu/cold relief, etc.). Put frequently used items at eye-level for easy access. Be sure your cabinet is kid-proof, especially if you have little ones.

5. **Dispose.** Bag and drop off expired and unused medications at a local drop-off point.

MEDICINE CABINET INSPIRATION

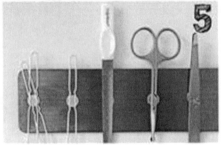

www.LivingWellSpendingLess.com

Photo Credit: Martha Stewart, Ikea, Real Simple, Container Store

Medicine Cabinet Inspiration
1. Clutter Free RX Cabinet (MarthaStewart.com)
2. Streamline 1st Aid Supplies (Ikea.com)
3. Prioritize People! (RealSimple.com)
4. Compartmentalize Tiny Spaces (ContainerStore.com)
5. Magnetize the Smalls (RealSimple.com)

Day 16 Checklist:

☐ Take a "before" photo
☐ Remove and put away any items that belong in other rooms.
☐ Remove all items from cabinet and any other areas to sort and declutter.
- ***Keep only items that:***
  - Are used by your family, both regularly and on occasion
  - Are unexpired
  - Actually do the trick
- ***Do not keep items that:***
  - Are expired, leaking or in broken containers
  - You no longer use or didn't fit your needs
  - Are over six months old
  - Need to be replaced.
☐ Thoroughly wipe down inside of cabinet.
☐ Line shelves with pretty paper.
☐ Create functional storage for your medicine cabinet. Organize like-items by shelf (daily vitamins, kids' medications, prescriptions, flu/cold relief, etc.). Put frequently used items at eye-level for easy access. Be sure your cabinet is kid-proof, especially if you have little ones. Use plastic bins or tiered shelf organizers so all items are easily accessible.
☐ Label any storage containers.
☐ Bag and discard expired and unwanted medications.
☐ Take an "after" photo and share on Instagram, Facebook, Pinterest, or Twitter with the hashtag #LWSLClutterFree!

$\mathcal{D}ay\,17$: Kids Bedrooms

Just like your master bedroom, a kid's bedroom should be a relaxing place for your child to get a restful sleep. Unlike the master bedroom, children's rooms often do double or even triple duty as their playroom and/or homework area. In a perfect world, each activity would have its own space, but often we have to make do with the space we have. Helping children divide their rooms into separate areas for each activity can help them become better sleepers, help them focus on homework, and even allow for more enriching playtime.

Kids' rooms can easily and quickly become a source of clutter and disorganization. Learning, discovering and growing can be, well, a messy job. Helping kids get a handle on their space can help them become more conscientious, better consumers, and more careful in the long run. Like all of us, your child's life can become overrun with "stuff," but paring down and clearing out clutter helps them feel more relaxed and in control of their space. It also helps them value their toys and belongings, so they gain a better appreciation for what they have.

If your children are old enough, let them take an active role in cleaning and organizing their own bedrooms. Review what activities they do in their bedroom and what's most important to them. This can foster some fascinating discussions and really spark some great connections with your child. Encourage them to donate rarely used items to charity—a local women and children's center, nursery or preschool can be a great option. Adding an altruistic spin on clearing out their clutter can bring enthusiasm and depth to the activity.

Objective: A child's bedroom that is clean and well organized with "a place for everything and everything in its place."

Assess the current situation: What do your children really use their bedroom for—Sleeping? Studying? Play? What items do they value and what are the treasures that make their room truly their own? Is there proper storage available for their bedroom activities? Is the bed kept clean, made and clutter free (including under-bed storage)?

Assignment:

1. **Remove and put away any items that belong in other rooms**. If necessary, use a basket to collect items, then distribute them to their proper homes.

2. **Sort everything!** Assess what your child truly enjoys and loves, and what has outlived its excitement.

   ### Keep only items that:
   - Are educational, stimulating, and loved by your child
   - Are in good repair and clean
   - Should be stored/housed in your child's bedroom

   ### Do not keep items that:
   - Are sentimental, but rarely played with
   - Have been outgrown or are no longer age-appropriate
   - Are broken, missing pieces or impossibly dirty

3. **Create distinct zones**. Designate areas in your child's room for sleep, play, and/or learning, as appropriate.

   - Sleep items include bed and bedding, a shelf of bedtime books, and one or two stuffed animals needed for bedtime.
   - Play items include learning or building toys, play sets, and items that can be housed or sorted into a type, such as Legos, action figures, dolls, play kitchen items, board games, etc. Each bunch should be sorted into a few bins that can be stored in allotted space.

- Learning items include a table, desk or writing surface, a desk chair, a computer, tablet, easel and art supplies. Sort these items into bins or containers as well and store in a cabinet, desk, or in drawers.

4. **Eliminate.** Purge all items that do not fit into the three categories you've designated, are no longer loved and used, or cannot be sorted and stored in the given space. Discard broken items and box or bag other items for donation.

5. **Label everything!** Label bins and storage containers clearly, using a label machine or even a snapshot glued to the outside of each bin. Everything should have a designated place. The more clearly your child can see where something goes, the more likely they are to return it to the proper place.

6. **Encourage good sleep hygiene**. Bedding should be clean and beds should be made each day. Beds should only be used for napping, sleeping and relaxation. Food, toys and electronics should never be brought into bed.

7. **Maintain.** Reassess the state of items in the room regularly with your child, as their interests change and they continue to learn and grow.

KIDS BEDROOM INSPIRATION

www.LivingWellSpendingLess.com

Photo Credit: Ikea, Container Store, BHG, Martha Stweart, Good House Keeping

Kids Bedroom Inspiration
1. Smarter Storage (www.GoodhouseKeeping.com)
2. Clever Kids Spaces (ContainerStore.com)
3. Rooms for Making Memories (Ikea.com)
4. Fresh Solutions for Kid Clutter (BHG.com)
5. Space Saver Desk (MarthaStewart.com)

Day 17 Checklist:

☐ Take a "before" photo
☐ Remove and put away any items that belong in other rooms.
☐ Clear all flat surfaces and gather items in one space to declutter.
- ***Keep only the items that:***
  - Fit into one of your three designated categories
  - Are calming, soothing and relaxing
  - Are currently useful
  - Are in good working order
  - Your child absolutely loves and wants to display
- ***Do NOT keep items that:***
  - Should be stored elsewhere
  - Interfere with your child's sleep
  - Causes anxiety or reduces your child's concentration
  - Your child does not use
  - Your child doesn't like
  - You feel obligated to keep because it was expensive
  - You feel obligated to keep because it was a gift
  - Are constantly in the way
☐ Create functional storage solutions for the items that you would like to keep in the room.
☐ Change bedding and replace if necessary.
☐ Remove any furniture that is no longer working for the space.
☐ Rearrange remaining furniture to make layout more functional and to designate more distinct areas for sleep, play, and study.

☐ Make subtle changes in lighting, sound, and décor to help create a more relaxing and soothing space for your child.

☐ Dust, sweep, vacuum, and clean glass surfaces.

☐ Label any storage containers.

☐ Immediately sell, toss, or donate unwanted items.

☐ Take an "after" photo and share on Instagram, Facebook, Pinterest, or Twitter with the hashtag #LWSLClutterFree!

Day 18: Kids Closet

Just as your master closet, kids' closets can come in many shapes and sizes. Adding to the variables is the fact that, like their closets, kids shapes and sizes are ever changing as well. At times it feels like kids can grow out of clothing as quickly as you buy it— not to mention stains, tears and taste in styles that change nearly as frequently.

A component of organizing is shopping wisely and planning ahead. Kids' closets are a prime example of this. Purchasing mix and match solid basics in wrinkle-free materials can help kids take an active role in not only planning their own outfits but in organizing and cleaning up after themselves. Not only that, but by purchasing smart easy-care fabrics, quality classic pieces, and separates that can work with in many combinations, you can get a lot of life out of children's clothing.

Enlisting your kids in the process of organizing their closet can be really fun. Ask them to try on items and get their opinions on what they like to wear. Purchase nice hangers, and limit children to the amount of clothing that fits on their hangers. Don't keep things that you are holding onto out of guilt or obligation, or because they were a gift. Allow these types of items to have new life by passing them on to consignment or Goodwill shops.

Objective: A kid's closet that is organized, accessible to them and filled with items they like to wear and feel good in.

Assess the current situation: What does your child feel most comfortable in? What fits, is free from wear, tear, stains and other damage? Can items be worn in several ways and with other pieces? How can items be arranged in a way that makes it easy for your child to access?

Assignment:

1. **Remove and put away any items that belong in other rooms.** If necessary, use a basket to collect items, then distribute them to their proper homes.

2. **Sort and declutter.** Go through clothing one piece at a time and divide into initial "keep," "discard" and "maybe" piles.

   ### Keep only items that:
   - Fit well and are age-appropriate
   - Your child likes and will wear
   - Are easy to care for and mix well in your child's wardrobe

   ### Do not keep items that:
   - No longer fit
   - You are holding onto out of guilt
   - Your child does not like or feels uncomfortable in
   - Cannot be worn in multiple outfits

3. **Organize your child's shoes.** Keep what fits comfortably and is in good repair. Wipe off the bottoms with a damp towel and put them into a shoe rack or shelf so each pair has its own spot.

4. **Reassess the piles.** Have your child try on the "keep" and "maybe" pile items to eliminate anything that does not properly fit.

5. **Hang.** Hang items by type, length and color into rows that can be easily reached by your kid. (You may need to move a closet bar down for frequently used items.)

6. **Fold.** Sort knits and separates into dresser drawers or on closet shelves, neatly folded and organized by color and type (jeans with jeans, t-shirts with t-shirts, etc.). Socks and underwear can be separated into clear plastic bins and rolled or organized into a drawer. Keep enough for a two-week rotation, getting rid of anything that is stained, worn out, or no-longer fits.

7. **Create a laundry solution.** Provide a ventilated hamper, basket or bin in or near the closet to help your child store laundry (rather than discarding it on the floor). Help your child take an active role in deciding where the hamper will go and what they think would work best.

KIDS CLOSET INSPIRATION

www.LivingWellSpendingLess.com

Kids Closet Inspiration
1. Neat & Tidy Nursery (EasyClosets.com)
2. Princess Packed Closet (ContainerStore.com)
3. Kid-Friendly Closet Ideas (BHG.com)
4. Within Reach (BHG.com)
5. Introduce Order (MarthaStewart.com)

Day 18 Checklist:

☐ Take a "before" photo
☐ Remove and put away any items that belong in other rooms.
☐ Assess each item of clothing in your child's closet and drawers—does it fit? Do they like it? Is it in good condition? Have they worn it in the last six months? Sort clothing into three piles—keep, donate and maybe.

- **Keep only items that:**
  - Fit well and are age-appropriate
  - Your child likes and will wear
  - Are easy to care for and mix well in your child's wardrobe
- **Do not keep items that:**
  - No longer fit
  - You are holding onto out of guilt
  - Your child does not like or feels uncomfortable in
  - Cannot be worn in multiple outfits

☐ Assess folded items using the same criteria.
☐ Organize your child's shoes, keeping what fits comfortably and is in good repair.
☐ Wipe off the bottom of each shoe with a damp towel and put them into a shoe rack or shelf so each pair has its own spot.
☐ Create functional storage for accessories
☐ Return clothing to closet and drawers, hanging clothing by type, length and color.
☐ Dust, sweep, vacuum, and clean glass surfaces.
☐ Label any storage containers.
☐ Provide a ventilated hamper.
☐ Immediately sell or donate unwanted items.
☐ Take an "after" photo and share on Instagram, Facebook, Pinterest, or Twitter with the hashtag #LWSLClutterFree!

$\mathcal{D}ay$ 19: Kids Paperwork

Children are wonderful, creative—and sometimes messy—little people. While none of us want to get rid of all that creativity, it can be hard to know exactly what to do with all that PAPER. As children reach school-age, bags come home filled with papers: permission slips, homework assignments, reading materials, report cards, and more—and it can all add up to a seemingly insurmountable mess.

Just like your desk at work or in your home office, paperwork should be constantly assessed and organized. It is also helpful to give your child a desk or designated area to store items that they are creating or working on. Hang a bulletin board in your child's room, or in your kitchen or family command center, and keep a designated box or spot for items that need immediate attention. Important work, projects and art can be displayed in a rotating gallery on the bulletin board. Items in the "immediate attention area" should be handled once and taken care of.

One of the best investments that parents can make is in a high quality scanner, though a more affordable option is to use a handy scanner app for iPhone or other smart phone. (I personally use and love the DocScanner Pro app!)

Once a month, or more frequently, sort through items that are on the bulletin board. "Masterpieces," Gold Star and A+ work can be scanned and archived after display. If your child is an aspiring artist, or voluminous writer, a portfolio or binder with sleeves can be a great way to archive their work. Encourage them to be discerning with what they choose to keep in its original format, and keep digital copies of the rest.

Objective: A paperwork system that fosters your child's creativity and celebrates their best work, while keeping work organized and accessible.

Assess the current situation: What items can be framed or are truly keepsakes? Do you have a system to take care of paperwork that needs your attention—a system that allows you to handle it once and move on? How can you electronically archive your kids' work to reduce clutter and access items as needed? What is your system for dealing with paperwork now? Do you review your child's backpack, homework and school communications daily?

Assignment:

1. **Collect and sort.** Gather all of the kid paperwork and art-work that may be floating around the house. Create an in-box in your family command center for permission slips and "need attention" items, and a spot on your child's desk or work area for homework and current projects. Select a few very special artwork items to keep for display, then scan any other items you want to remember but not necessarily keep.

2. **Review.** Plan a weekly review system for younger children and nightly for older children, to assess the contents of your child's backpack, communication from daycare, school and preschool, artwork and creative projects.

3. **Take immediate action.** Handle items such as permission slips as soon as they come in and return them to school the very next day.

4. **Enjoy and celebrate.** Display artwork on a bulletin board, and once a month scan and archive great work.

5. **Archive.** Create a portfolio, binder, or special box for cre-ative projects and keepsakes that can be stored and reviewed, as your child gets older.

KIDS PAPERWORK INSPIRATION

1. Color Coded Clutter Free Zone (Clean-Organized-Family-Home.com)
2. Smart Ideas For Family Organizing (BHG.com)
3. A Place To Study (KidSpaceStuff.com)
4. Craft Project Storage (MarthaStewart.com)
5. School Paperwork Storage (IHeartOrganizing.BlogSpot.com)

Day 19 Checklist:

- ☐ Take a "before" photo
- ☐ Collect all kid paperwork and artwork and bring to a central location.
- ☐ Sort all paperwork into action items (homework, permission slips, etc.), artwork to display, artwork to scan and toss, and keepsakes.
- ☐ Create an inbox for your family control center that can be used to collect important action items.
- ☐ Hang display items on a bulletin board or other display area.
- ☐ Scan remaining artwork, then discard.
- ☐ Create an archive binder or box for keepsake items. If you have more than one child, create a separate box or binder for each child.
- ☐ Begin checking your child's backpack daily for incoming paperwork and artwork.
- ☐ Schedule a scanning session once a month.
- ☐ Label any storage containers.
- ☐ Immediately toss unwanted items.
- ☐ Take an "after" photo and share on Instagram, Facebook, Pinterest, or Twitter with the hashtag #LWSLClutterFree!

$\mathcal{D}ay$ 20: **Kids Bathroom**

Children, especially girls, can have a shocking amount of bathroom accessories. Hair ties, ponytail holders, bows, nail polish, sunscreen and other products can overflow bathroom counters and drawers in no time. Add in teens or multiple kids sharing a bathroom and that is a lot of clutter!

Giving each child a designated bin or shower caddy can be a lifesaver, and storing these designated bins in a nearby linen closet if possible can also be extremely helpful. You can also make room under the sink or even by assigning each family member a drawer for non-shower items, plus a plastic basket for shampoo, razors and other shower items. Plastic storage bins that can be easily cleaned and stacked are great for makeup, nail polish, hair accessories and more.

It's easy to hoard bathroom products and you may suddenly find that your daughter's Lip Smacker collection has taken over every area of the house, or that her hair bands wind up everywhere, even somehow in the cat bowl. Encourage kids to buy and keep only what they can use in six months. Most beauty products don't keep beyond that time: hairspray and products breakdown the rubber in elastics and gum up hair bows and headbands, making them unusable in the long-term. If something is past its prime, let it go.

Objective: An organized bathroom for use by multiple family members or multiple genders and age groups.

Assess the current situation: Does each user have appropriate storage space? Are you utilizing storage space efficiently? Can items be stored and pared down so countertops are clear and so the shower and tub can dry, staying clean and mildew free?

Assignment:

1. **Remove and put away any items that belong in other rooms.** If necessary, use a basket to collect items, then distribute them to their proper homes.

2. **Sort and declutter.** Remove all items from drawers and under-sink cabinets, and off the vanity and other areas. Assign a pile for each person. Discard anything that has not been used within the last three months. Check all expiration dates and discard anything that is over six months old. (Again, lotion can separate, and sunscreen and other products lose effectiveness and can even go rancid.)

   Keep only items that:
   - Are used regularly
   - Fit in each person's allotted storage container or space
   - Are in good repair

   Do not keep items that:
   - Are expired, leaking or in broken containers
   - Are over six months old
   - Are sensitive to heat or moisture (like medications)

3. **Clean.** Thoroughly wipe down all surfaces, insides of drawers and cabinets and shower surfaces.

4. **Organize.** Sort "like" items together—for example: hair products and accessories, shower products, and under-sink storage items.

5. **Beautify.** If you like, line drawers with pretty paper or drawer liners.

6. **Create functional storage areas in your drawers and cabinets.** Use lidded clear plastic containers to house smaller items in drawers. Organize larger bottles in plastic crates with drainage for storage under the sink. Separate them into large plastic bags and label with markers. Toilet paper, feminine hygiene items and other products can be stored under the sink.

7. **Organize shower and bath products into a drainable, portable caddy.** Each person should have their own caddy to eliminate shower clutter and mildew. Hang a squeegee in your shower and spray for quick cleaning after each use.

8. **Take special care of hair accessories, nail polish and makeup:**

   - Wipe off each item with a damp towel
   - Assign each item its own bin or lidded container
   - Discard anything separated, broken or dirty
   - Keep only items that fit in the bin.
   - Hair bows and accessories may be better stored in a closet on a special hanger or organizer
   - Reassess items frequently—most open cosmetics expire after 6 months

KIDS BATHROOM INSPIRATION

www.LivingWellSpendingLess.com

Kids Bathroom Inspiration
1. Squeaky Clean Storage Inspiration (Bed-Bath.HomexGarden.com)
2. Cube Style & Function (HomeGoods.com)
3. Bath-Time baskets (DecoratingIdeas4KidsRooms.com)
4. Tucked Away Bath Toys (HomeDIT.com)
5. Big Ideas For Bathrooms (DIYNetwork.com)

Day 20 Checklist:

- ☐ Take a "before" photo
- ☐ Remove and put away any items that belong in other rooms.
- ☐ Remove all items from drawers, under-sink cabinets, vanity and other areas to sort and declutter.
  - *Keep only items that:*
    - Are used regularly
    - Fit in each person's allotted storage container or space
    - Are in good condition or repair
  - *Do not keep items that:*
    - Are expired, leaking or in broken containers
    - You no longer use or didn't fit your needs
    - Are over six months old
    - Are sensitive to heat or moisture (like medications)
    - Are decorative but difficult to keep clean
- ☐ Thoroughly wipe down all surfaces, insides of drawers and cabinets, and shower surfaces.
- ☐ Create functional storage areas in drawers and cabinets. Use lidded clear plastic containers to house smaller items in drawers. Organize larger bottles in plastic crates with drainage for storage under the sink. Separate them into large plastic bags and label with markers. Toilet paper, feminine hygiene items and other products can be stored under the sink.
- ☐ Organize shower and bath products into a drainable caddy
- ☐ Hang a squeegee in your shower and spray for quick cleaning after each use.

☐ Dust, sweep, vacuum, and clean glass surfaces.

☐ Label any storage containers.

☐ Immediately toss or donate unwanted items.

☐ Take an "after" photo and share on Instagram, Facebook, Pinterest, or Twitter with the hashtag #LWSLClutterFree!

$\mathcal{D}$ay 21: Laundry Room and Linen Closet

Linen closets and laundry rooms can be elusive spaces. Some older homes simply have a hallway cupboard, washer and dryer in the garage, or nothing at all, while newer homes offer walk-in linen closets and large utility rooms full of space. Some linen closets may do double-duty as storage for vacuum, laundry and cleaning items, while others are dedicated to simply linens.

Whatever your laundry and linen space, keeping it neat organized will help you to be a more efficient housekeeper. Your laundry room should be a space that helps you complete your laundry more efficiently, while your linen closet should help keep all those freshly washed and neatly folded sheets and towels ready for use.

Traditionally only things such as sheets, towels and table linens are housed in the linen closet, but you may find that it also becomes the overflow storage for shower caddies, bathroom supplies, cleaning supplies, toilet paper and paper towels. Ultimately your success in decluttering and organizing this area will come down to paring your supplies down to the barest essentials.

Objective: A fresh, neat area to do laundry, store sheets, towels, and a "pantry" for cleaning and bathroom supplies.

Assess the current situation: How much space do you have? Are there items that need to be stored beyond towels and sheets? How many cleaning and laundry products do you have? Do you use them all? What changes could you make to create more space?

Assignment:

1. **Remove and put away any items that belong in other rooms.** If necessary, use a basket to collect items, then distribute them to their proper homes.

2. **Sort and declutter.** Remove all items from the closet and cupboards. Spray and wipe out shelves and line with shelf paper. Toss any cleaning supplies or products that are not being used or no longer any good. Limit cleaning and laundry supplies to the bare minimum.

3. **Keep two sets of sheets per bed**—the one on the bed and a spare, which should be rotated and laundered once a week. Discard sheets when they become worn. Sheet sets should be folded together—folding the flat sheet into the fitted sheet with one pillowcase and placing the set inside the second pillowcase. This method of folding makes it easy to grab the entire set and keep it together.

4. **Keep no more than three bath sheets and three hand towels per person.** Discard any towels that are frayed or thinning. Fold bath towels in fourths and then thirds, turning the edge inward when stacking for a uniform look.

5. **Organize paper items.** Store paper towels, tissue and toilet paper on higher shelves, stacking neatly.

6. **Organize remaining cleaning and laundry products.** Sort cleaning items, extra unopened bath products and other items on lower shelves, by first sorting and storing smaller like-items in clear, labeled plastic bags, and then storing with larger items in plastic bins.

LAUNDRY & LINEN INSPIRATION

www.LivingWellSpendingLess.com

Photo Credit: Container Store, BHG, Family Circle, Martha Stewart

Laundry & Linen Inspiration
1. Streamlined Laundry Room (ContainersStore.com)
2. Customized Linen Closet (BHG.com)
3. Optimize Unused Door Space (FamilyCircle.com)
4. Everything in it's Place (MarthaStwewart.com)
5. Organized Bed Linens (MarthaStwewart.com)

𝒟ay 21 Checklist:

- ☐ Take a "before" photo
- ☐ Remove and put away any items that belong in other rooms.
- ☐ Remove all items from drawers, under-sink cabinets, cupboards, closets, and other areas to sort and declutter.
  - *Keep only linens, laundry and cleaning products that:*
    - ▪ Are used regularly
    - ▪ Are in good condition or repair
  - *Do not keep items that:*
    - ▪ Are expired, leaking or in broken containers
    - ▪ You no longer use or didn't fit your needs
    - ▪ Are over one year old
    - ▪ Are decorative but difficult to keep clean
    - ▪ Are worn, threadbare, or full of holes.
- ☐ Thoroughly wipe down all surfaces, insides of drawers and cabinets, and washer/dryer units.
- ☐ Create functional storage areas in drawers and cabinets. Use lidded clear plastic containers to house smaller items in drawers. Organize larger bottles in plastic crates with drainage for storage under the sink.
- ☐ Keep two sets of sheet per bed; replace worn linens if necessary.
- ☐ Keep three bath towels, three hand towels, and three washcloths per family member. Reserve a few old towels to use as rags, if needed; otherwise toss old or worn towels.

- ☐ Return neatly folded sheets and towels to linen closet; create storage for large, bulky, or paper items, if necessary.
- ☐ Dust, sweep, vacuum, and clean glass surfaces.
- ☐ Label any storage containers.
- ☐ Immediately toss or donate unwanted items.
- ☐ Take an "after" photo and share on Instagram, Facebook, Pinterest, or Twitter with the hashtag #LWSLClutterFree!

$\mathcal{D}ay$ 22: Home Office

While working from has become much more common these days, everyone—especially those whose primary task is to manage the goings-on of a busy family—needs a functional space to take care of your bills, budget, and schedule. Even if you love your job, work is still *work*, and creating a cheery, inviting space to perform that work not only uplifts your spirit but helps increase productivity.

Find or recycle containers to create desk organizers (a little paint, washi tape and pretty paper can go a long way). Hang some art, put in a plant and do your best to beautify your workspace. It can work wonders for creativity and productivity!

Finally, designate a space for everything and sort it before it hits the desk: address daily, address monthly, file/archive. Keep your checkbook, stamps, labels and other tools at your fingertips so something important won't get so easily pushed off into the "deal with it later" pile. Ten minutes of proactive organization a day can transform your procrastination into productivity.

Objective: A beautiful and inviting workspace where you can address work quickly and efficiently.

Assess the current situation: Does your home office provide you with the space you need? Is this an area you can work in? Are there items there that are unnecessary for the space?

Assignment:

1. **Remove and put away any items that belong in other rooms.** If necessary, use a basket to collect items, then distribute them to their proper homes.

2. **Collect loose papers.** Put all paperwork in an out-of-the-way area to be addressed in tomorrow's challenge.

3. **Sort and declutter.** Empty, sort and organize all desk drawers using small containers or boxes. Keep only office supplies and items that you use frequently or can use up in the course of a year. (Try donating excess supplies to a school, church or other charity.)

4. **Organize office supplies into containers.** Put only frequently used items on the desktop, and all others should be housed inside the desk. A paper sorter or file area should be easily accessible. Include a mail center or drawer with stamps, envelopes and blank stationary.

5. **Dust and clean.** Wipe down dusty areas and use compressed air to clean the back of your computer, keyboard and hard-to-reach areas. Fully wipe down your desk chair, shelves, windowsills, and any other areas that may be collecting dirt or grime. Sweep & vacuum as well.

6. **Organize cords**, using zip ties or clips and labeling each.

7. **Hang a bulletin board.** Use this to house clippings, photos and inspirational items.

8. **Decorate & beautify**. Consider adding a plant, relaxing pictures, or other items to warm the space and make it relaxing and inviting. However, be careful not to add in new clutter after taking it away—instead be very intentional about what you allow in this space. Finally, make sure your chair is comfortable and ergonomic and that the space is well-lit and easy to navigate.

HOME OFFICE INSPIRATION

www.LivingWellSpendingLess.com

Photo Credit: Container Store, Real Simple,
Home DIT, Martha Stewart

Home Office Inspiration
1. Home Office Simplified (ContainersStore.com)
2. Double Duty Decorating (RealSimple.Com)
3. Cozy Creative Office Space (HomeDIT.com)
4. Organizing Your Home Office (ContainersStore.com)
5. Desk Job (MarthaStwewart.com)

Day 22 Checklist:

☐ Take a "before" photo

☐ Remove and put away any items that belong in other rooms.

☐ Collect loose papers and put all paperwork in an out-of-the-way area to be addressed in tomorrow's challenge.

☐ Remove all items from drawers, cabinets, your desk-top, and other areas to sort and declutter.

- *Keep only items that:*
  - Are used regularly
  - Are in good condition or repair
- *Do not keep items that:*
  - Are broken or don't work
  - You no longer use or didn't fit your needs
  - Are decorative but difficult to keep clean
  - You are afraid to get rid of because they are expensive
  - You are afraid to get rid of because they were a gift
  - You don't like

☐ Thoroughly clean all surfaces, insides of drawers and cupboards, shelves and top of desk. Wipe down dusty areas and use compressed air to clean the back of your computer, keyboard and hard-to-reach areas. Fully wipe down your desk chair, shelves, win-dowsills, and any other areas that may be collecting dirt or grime.

☐ Create functional storage areas in drawers and cabi-nets. Put only frequently used items on the desktop, and all others should be housed inside the desk. A paper sorter or file area should be easily accessible.

- ☐ Create a mail center or drawer with stamps, envelopes and blank stationary
- ☐ Organize cords, using zip ties or clips and labeling each.
- ☐ Hang a bulletin board.
- ☐ Sweep, vacuum, and clean glass surfaces.
- ☐ Label any storage containers.
- ☐ Immediately toss or donate unwanted items.
- ☐ Take an "after" photo and share on Instagram, Facebook, Pinterest, or Twitter with the hashtag #LWSLClutterFree!

$\mathcal{D}ay$ 23: Bills and Paperwork

Home office and desk areas can easily become number one clutter-catchers. With multiple family members congregating around a single home computer, this zone can quickly become the eye of a paper clutter hurricane. While we have already worked on creating workable systems for mail and children's paperwork, it is also important to make sure your home has a functional system for all bills and additional paperwork that come through your door.

One important key to cutting down the clutter is having a strong filing system. If you can, let go of the need to have paper and tangible files. Scan and archive as much as you can and switch to online bill-paying to cut back on junk mail and paperwork. When mail arrives, open and sort it immediately, keeping a waste bin nearby so you can discard junk then and there. Use electronic subscriptions for magazines so you can read them from your tablet and cut back on even more paper.

It can be difficult to "let go" of paper. Scanning and archiving can take some getting used to. Once you start to cut back on paper, you will be amazed at how much freer and in control you feel.

Objective: A bill-pay, paperwork and filing system that keeps your home office clear of clutter and user-friendly.

Assess the current situation: How much space do you need for files? What can be shredded and discarded? How can you cut back on paper?

Assignment:

1. **Sort and declutter.** Gather the paperwork compiled from yesterday's office organization plus any other paperwork still lying around the house in order to sort and declutter.

    ### Sort into the following piles:
    - Can be resolved now
    - Junk/remove from list
    - Can be changed to online payment/statement now
    - Can be resolved in two weeks
    - Can be resolved in one month
    - Can be scanned and archived
    - Can be filed
    - Can be shredded

    ### Scan the following:
    - Paid invoices for one year (change as many as possible to online bill-pay)
    - Receipts for one year
    - Articles, clippings and inspirations
    - Medical receipts, claims and informational documents
    - Car repair info and receipts

    ### File the following:
    - Taxes and correspondence with the IRS (save for seven years and then shred)
    - Legal claims and documents
    - Business licenses and legal documents, such as articles of incorporation
    - Social Security statements/cards, birth certificates, titles and licenses (store in a secure location, in a safe or safety deposit box)

2. **Switch to online bill pay**. Contact all of the entities that send you a monthly bill and find out if they offer online bill pay. Insurance companies and investment firms almost always offer e-statements. Contact yours and switch.

3. **Eliminate junk mail.** If you didn't do this already on Day Three, contact all junk mail senders and ask to be removed from their list. Discard junk mail immediately (before it ever hits your desk or any other surface in your home).

4. **Bank online.** If you don't have it already, set up online banking and request electronic statements.

5. **Shred and discard.** Get rid of all items that are no longer relevant.

Bills & Paperwork Inspiration

www.LivingWellSpendingLess.com

Entryway Inspiration
1. Paint-Can Bill Pay Center (MarthaStwewart.com)
2. Desktop Priority Station (ContainerStore.com)
3. Put your Walls to Work (BHG.com)
4. Family Command Center (RealSimple.Com)
5. Bills Front & Center (BHG.com)

Day 23 Checklist:

☐ Take a "before" photo
☐ Gather all paperwork to sort and declutter
   Sort into the following piles:
   - Can be resolved now
   - Junk/remove from list
   - Can be changed to online payment/statement now
   - Can be resolved in two weeks
   - Can be resolved in one month
   - Can be scanned and archived
     - *Paid invoices for one year (change as many as possible to online bill-pay)*
     - *Receipts for one year*
     - *Articles, clippings and inspirations*
     - *Medical receipts, claims and informational documents*
     - *Car repair info and receipts*
   - Can be filed
     - *Taxes and correspondence with the IRS (save for seven years and then shred)*
     - *Legal claims and documents*
     - *Business licenses and legal documents, such as articles of incorporation*
     - *Social Security statements/cards, birth certificates, titles and licenses (store in a secure location, in a safe or safety deposit box)*
   - Can be shredded

☐ Switch to online bill pay. Contact all of the entities that send you a monthly bill and find out if they offer online bill pay. Insurance companies and investment firms almost always offer e-statements. Contact yours and switch.

☐ Eliminate junk mail. If you didn't do this already on Day Three, contact all junk mail senders and ask to be removed from their list. Discard junk mail immediately (before it ever hits your desk or any other surface in your home).

☐ Bank online. If you don't have it already, set up online banking and request electronic statements.

☐ Label any storage containers.

☐ Shred and discard unwanted items.

☐ Take an "after" photo and share on Instagram, Facebook, Pinterest, or Twitter with the hashtag #LWSLClutterFree!

$\mathcal{D}ay$ 24: **Digital Data**

By now you should be used to the idea of digital scanning and document archiving. Like most people, you probably also have a number of files and archives already on your computer, such as digital photos, videos, and the like. Depending on your computer use and the amount of data you've stored, you may prefer to address digital clutter in one of several different ways.

For simplicity's sake, we will start with basic digital organization. There are many cloud-based programs that can help store your files, depending on how tech-savvy you are and how much storage space you need. If you find yourself needing more storage than your basic home computer can offer, then it is time to start researching storage options; consider an external hard drive.

The average home computer user may simply need a solution to sort files in a way they can be quickly found when needed. It can be overwhelming, especially if you have simply "saved" items willy-nilly all over your desktop, in your My Documents folder, on a thumb drive, and/or in your email attachments. If you find yourself afraid to empty your "recycle bin" on your computer because you've used it as an archive system, you know you have a problem.

Think of your hard drive as a basic filing cabinet. Each user should have their own profile, or at minimum, their own folder. If you are concerned about how your children access your files and/or if privacy is a major concern, parents may want to install a safe browser, share a family login, and monitor and limit kids' computer time.

Objective: A digital data filing system that works for a family's basic needs on a shared home computer.

Assess the current situation: How many people use your computer? Do you have a file folder for each user? How can those files be broken down in a way that is most useful to you? How can you sort and access digital data in a quick, non-overwhelming way?

Assignment:

1. **Make a plan.** Write a list of all of the digital items you store on your computer. For example:

    -   Bills to pay
    -   Paid bills/invoices (consider sorting by vendor)
    -   Monthly statements (consider sorting by vendor)
    -   Photographs (sort by month)
    -   Scanned photos/homework/artwork
    -   Scanned receipts
    -   Writing, journals, etc.
    -   Home budget

2. **Create folders.** Each user of a particular computer should have their own folder on the hard drive. Furthermore, you should create folders for each of the categories listed above, as well as any sub categories. If you like to keep your folders on your desktop, consider installing a desktop background that can help you sort your folders. I love this free desktop background from Heather Moritz at Moritz Fine Designs: http://www.moritzfineblogdesigns.com/2013/08/clean-up-your-computer-desktop-simple-computer-organization/

3. **Sort your files.** Drag files to the appropriate sorting folders, then drag folders into "My Documents" or whichever file you've designated as home base.

4. **Protect your files.** Consider a password storage program or app like LastPass or RoboForm to protect your passwords and data.

5. **Streamline your online data.** Clear out any bookmarks in your browser you no longer use. Consider using a program

or app like Feedly to manage your news, blogs and RSS feeds.

6. **Back up your files.** Determine how you will access all your files in the event of an emergency. (If all your kid pictures live on your desktop computer, you need a backup system NOW. How would you feel if you lost all those precious memories?) Save files to an external hard drive or memory stick, or install an automatic digital backup program like Mozy. It is also not a bad idea to back up your files in multiple locations. If you have a safe deposit box, copy your photos once a year onto a memory stick to store in your box.

DIGITAL DATA INSPIRATION

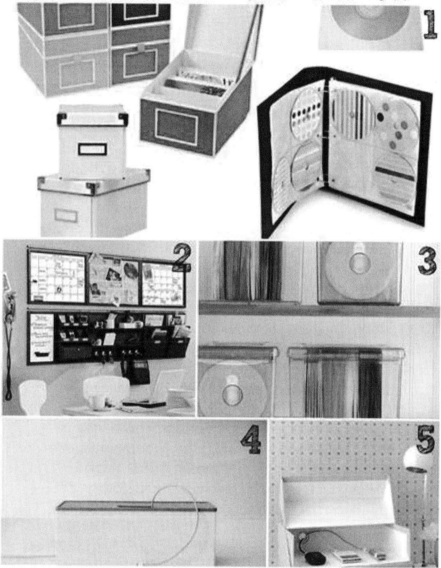

www.LivingWellSpendingLess.com

Photo Credit: Container Store, Ikea
Creative Home Idea, Martha Stewart

Digital Data Inspiration
1. Take The Boring Out of Storing (ContainerStore.com)
2. Digital Device Display (CreativeHomeIdea.com)
3. Color Coded CD & DVD Display (ContainerStore.com)
4. Organize This & That (Ikea.com)
5. DIY Charging Dock Blueprint (MarthaStwewart.com)

Day 24 Checklist:

☐ Take a "before" photo of your messy desktop.

☐ Make a plan. Write a list of all of the digital items you store on your computer. For example:
- Bills to pay
- Paid bills/invoices (consider sorting by vendor)
- Monthly statements (consider sorting by vendor)
- Photographs (sort by month)
- Scanned photos/homework/artwork
- Scanned receipts
- Writing, journals, etc.
- Home budget

☐ Create folders. Each user of a particular computer should have their own folder on the hard drive. Furthermore, you should create folders for each of the categories listed above, as well as any sub categories. If you like to keep your folders on your desktop, consider installing a desktop background that can help you sort your folders.

☐ Sort your files. Drag files to the appropriate sorting folders, then drag folders into "My Documents" or whichever file you've designated as home base.

☐ Protect your files. Consider a password storage program or app like LastPass or RoboForm to protect your passwords and data.

☐ Streamline your online data. Clear out any bookmarks in your browser you no longer use. Consider using a program or app like Feedly to manage your news, blogs and RSS feeds.

☐ Back up your files. Determine how you will access all your files in the event of an emergency. Save files to an external hard drive or memory stick, or install an automatic digital backup program like Mozy. It is also not a bad idea to back up your files in multiple locations.

☐ If you have a safe deposit box, copy your important files once a year onto a memory stick to store in your box.

☐ Take an "after" photo of your organized desktop and share on Instagram, Facebook, Pinterest, or Twitter with the hashtag #LWSLClutterFree!

$\mathcal{D}ay$ 25: **Photographs**

Believe it or not, but in the last six months, the number of photos taken by the human race has actually *doubled*. This is an amazing and staggering statistic. With the advent of social media and digital photography, it's time to rethink how we archive and store our photos. The problem of yesterday—how to archive paper photos in acid-free storage—is nearly extinct. Now the problem becomes how to label and sort through files of photographs in a way that makes them accessible so they can be shared and enjoyed.

Paper photographs can, and should be, arranged chronologically and eventually scanned into digital files. Not only will this help keep them organized, but it can prevent tragedy from destroying valued memories. Storing photos in archival quality photo boxes (sorted by year) can help ensure that your family will enjoy them and that they are accessible for scrapbooking and other projects.

Digital photography, on the other hand, can be a different beast to tame. One of the main tendencies is to hold on to too many files. While it can be hard to part with even one baby picture, hanging on to the not-so-great shots can make sorting and storing them a difficult chore.

Keep the photos that you deem good to excellent. Use an online service such as Picasa, Snapfish, iPhoto, Flickr or Photobucket. Organize the photos by year, month, and then event, such as "2014 May Jenny Birthday Party Cake." It may seem like an arduous process, but adding a descriptor can really ensure that you will be able to easily find photos for later use. Commit to uploading photos once a month and the task will seem less daunting as you go. Many online services offer great printable gifts and beautiful keepsake photo books as well.

Objective: Organized files of both film and digital photography.

Assess the current situation: What is your current storage method? How can photos be organized? How can photos be digitally organized and archived?

Assignment:

1. **Sort and declutter your printed photographs.** Gather all your print photos and organize into piles by year. Toss any that aren't very good, then sort the rest into stackable acid-free photo boxes.

2. **Organize your digital photos.** Using the following guidelines to sort and declutter:

   - Upload any photos that are on your phone or camera
   - Keep only the best photos
   - Organize onto an online photo storage program
   - Rename files in a logical manner by date and event
   - Scan, name and archive film photographs, starting with the oldest first

PHOTO STORAGE INSPIRATION

www.LivingWellSpendingLess.com

Photo Credit: Container Store, Woman's Day, BHG, SnapFish, Martha Stewart

Photo Storage Inspiration
1. Photo Storage Carrier (ContainerStore.com)
2. Keep Precious Memories on Instant Recall (BHG.com)
3. Organize Your Photos Like A Pro (WomansDay.com)
4. Snappy Digital Storage (SnapFish.com)
5. Instant Photo Album(MarthaStwewart.com)

Day 25 Checklist:

☐ Take a "before" photo

☐ Gather all your print photos and organize into piles by year.

☐ Toss any photos that are not very good, only keeping the best shot of multiples. If you have a lot of photos, be ruthless about what you throw away. There is no benefit to keeping too many photographs.

☐ Sort remaining photographs into stackable acid-free photo boxes.

☐ Organize your digital photos. Using the following guidelines to sort and declutter:

- Upload any photos that are on your phone or camera

- Keep only the best photos. Again, be ruthless about what you keep! If you took ten photos of the same shot, keep only the very best one.

- Rename files in a logical manner by date and event

- Scan, name and archive film photographs, starting with the oldest first

☐ Create folders for each year to store digital photo files.

☐ Sort your files. Drag files to the appropriate sorting folders.

☐ Back up your files.

☐ If you have a safe deposit box, copy your photos once a year onto a memory stick to store in your box.

☐ Take an "after" photo of your organized desktop and share on Instagram, Facebook, Pinterest, or Twitter with the hashtag #LWSLClutterFree!

$\mathcal{D}ay$ 26: Guest Room

Not everyone is lucky enough to have a guest room, but nearly everyone is lucky enough to have guests! Whether it's providing a couch for a friend in need or a room for a relative who's coming to town, there are a few things that can be done to ensure your guest has a warm, safe, inviting space to make them feel right at home.

There are a few universal courtesies that all guests will appreciate. Integrating each into your guest room is a must and will really brighten their stay—plus, the care you take will ensure your hospitality won't go unnoticed.

Even if you have an extra bedroom that is solely for guests, chances are a few other things migrate to that space as well. If your home is anything like mine, your guest room is also one of the only extra storage areas in the home! Many guest rooms, by necessity, become overflow centers for storage, bins of Christmas decorations, closets full of dance recital dresses and items that aren't used often, but can't quite be parted with just yet, either.

Take the time to truly consider this space and how you most want it to be used. If possible, move storage to the attic, basement and garage, or better yet, consider if the items are even needed at all. If the room serves a dual purpose, investing in a daybed, pullout couch or futon can help maximize the space. Keeping things organized and clean can ensure that your guests, when they arrive, aren't tripping over your treadmill or fighting cat allergies during their stay.

Objective: A welcoming space for guests that meets their needs and doesn't "collect dust" when they are not there.

Assess the current situation: Do you have frequent guests? What purpose does the space serve when you do not have guests? How can you make the space inviting? Are things housed in the space that could be stored elsewhere?

Assignment:

1. **Remove and put away any items that belong in other rooms**. If necessary, use a basket to collect items, then distribute them to their proper homes.

2. **Assess the space and its current use.** Remove all items that cannot be attractively stored in an organized manner.

3. **Sort, declutter, and store remaining items.** Try to arrange any items that must be stored in this room to be as minimally invasive to guests as possible. Get rid of anything that is not absolutely essential, or anything you can bear to part with. After a nearly a month of decluttering, you should be getting pretty good at this job!

4. **Prepare for guests.** Set up guest room amenities so they're all ready to go when your guests arrive.

   A great guest room provides:
   - A comfortable, clean place to sleep with extra blankets/bedding (fold and store at the foot of the bed or in a closet)
   - An accessible outlet for a phone charger (and your Wi-Fi password)
   - A nightstand with a light and somewhere to hold a glass of water
   - Welcoming, clean décor and space to put a suitcase or bag
   - Freedom from allergen-triggers (Fido should sleep elsewhere), loud noises and bright lights
   - Access to a bathroom with a towel and basic amenities

An outstanding guest room provides

- A snack, fruit or nosh for the midnight-snacker
- An extra toothbrush, hand lotion, face wipes and reading material (store in the nightstand)
- Privacy and solace
- Flowers, plants, candles and other welcoming touches

GUEST BEDROOM INSPIRATION

Photo Credit: West Elm, BHG, Martha Stewart

Guest Bedroom Inspiration
1. Clever Clean-Lined Room (WestElm.com)
2. Under The Bed Drawers (MarthaStewart.com)
3. Bedtime Bookshelf (BHG.com)
4. New Neutrals Guest Room (WestElm.com)
5. Space Smarts (BHG.com)

Day 26 Checklist:

☐ Take a "before" photo
☐ Remove and put away any items that belong in other rooms.
☐ Assess the space and its current use. Remove all items that cannot be attractively stored in an organized manner.
☐ Sort, declutter, and store remaining items. Try to arrange any items that must be stored in this room to be as minimally invasive to guests as possible. Get rid of anything that is not absolutely essential, or anything you can bear to part with.
☐ Thoroughly clean all surfaces, insides of drawers and cupboards, shelves and tops of dressers. Fully wipe down your desk chair, shelves, windowsills, and any other areas that may be collecting dirt or grime.
☐ Create functional storage areas in drawers, cabinets, and closets.
☐ Sweep, vacuum, and clean glass surfaces.
☐ Label any storage containers.
☐ Prepare for guests. Set up guest room amenities so they're all ready to go when your guests arrive.

A great guest room provides:

- A comfortable, clean place to sleep with extra blankets/bedding (fold and store at the foot of the bed or in a closet)
- An accessible outlet for a phone charger (and your Wi-Fi password)
- A nightstand with a light and somewhere to hold a glass of water
- Welcoming, clean décor and space to put a suitcase or bag

- Freedom from allergen-triggers (Fido should sleep elsewhere), loud noises and bright lights
- Access to a bathroom with a towel and basic amenities

An outstanding guest room provides

- A snack, fruit or nosh for the midnight-snacker
- An extra toothbrush, hand lotion, face wipes and reading material (store in the nightstand)
- Privacy and solace
- Flowers, plants, candles and other welcoming touches

☐ Immediately toss or donate unwanted items.
☐ Take an "after" photo and share on Instagram, Facebook, Pinterest, or Twitter with the hashtag #LWSLClutterFree!

$\mathcal{D}ay$ 27: Craft Supplies

Indulging your creative side can be both fun and relaxing. Crafting, painting, and even gardening and other such hobbies provide a welcome respite from daily life. Not only that, but they give an outlet for creativity, allowing us to learn and grow and to beautify the world around us.

Unfortunately the supplies used to undertake these creative hobbies can be small, easily scattered, hard to organize, strangely shaped and difficult to store. Some of us are craft addicts and tend to purchase truckloads of tools, supplies and items as we hone our skills at each new craft. It can be hard to part with craft supplies and tools because many are pricy and often there is some guilty or a "never say die" mentality, even when we've undertaken projects that we admittedly don't love.

One of the key factors to organizing a craft area, whatever that space may be, is knowing when to say enough is enough. Perhaps you tried knitting, but have a half-made, lumpy scarf still on the needles, and 10 skeins of yarn in a basket. Perhaps you made Christmas ornaments two years ago and still have bags of pompoms and rickrack that you just can't quite get rid of. Give yourself permission to let it go.

Reusable items can be donated to schools or afterschool programs. Other items, like fleece, can be cut into small "cage comforters" and donated to your local animal shelter. Think creatively about who might really get some use out of the abandoned items and pass them on!

Once you've let go, focus on the crafts that you truly love and feel good doing. Organize your supplies and let your creativity take off! You'll be surprised at how free you will feel once you give yourself permission to create things you are proud of.

Objective: Organized craft supplies that are frequently used with a storage solution.

Assess the current situation: What craft activities do you really love to do? What items are you holding onto out of guilt? Who can use the items? What does your storage space look like? How can you effectively store the items and make a useful workspace?

Assignment:

1. **Remove and put away any items that belong in other rooms.** If necessary, use a basket to collect items, then distribute them to their proper homes.

2. **Sort and declutter.** Gather all craft supplies. Sort them by type (adhesives, papers, fabric, cutting implements, etc.), and by project.

   ### Keep only items that:
   - You have used for a project in the last year
   - You enjoy working with and feel good about
   - You have enough of, to be used for a solidified future project (not scraps)
   - Can fit within a designated craft/storage area

   ### Do not keep items that:
   - You are keeping out of guilt
   - Were used for a completed project and can't be used for a concrete project in the future
   - Are damaged or will not be used in the future

3. **Let go!** Purge all items that do not fit into the keep category or those that cannot be sorted and stored in the given space. Discard broken items and box or bag other items for donation.

4. **Clean your crafting area.** Wipe down shelves, cupboards, and drawers. Sweep, vacuum, and clean glass surfaces.

5. **Create functional storage solutions for all your craft supplies.** Look on Pinterest or other resources within your own hobby genre for creative storage solution ideas that fit the needs for your particular passion.

6. **Label everything!** Take the time to clearly label bins and storage containers, using labels or even a Polaroid-type picture on the outside of each bin. Everything should have a designated place.

CRAFT STORAGE INSPIRATION

www.LivingWellSpendingLess.com

Photo Credit: Container Store, BHG, Good House keeping

Craft Storage Inspiration
1. Deluxe Craft Center (ContainerStore.com)
2. The Perfect Craft Cabinet (BHG.com)
3. Kids Crafting Corner (ContainerStore.com)
4. Cute & Clever Craft Organizing (BHG.com)
5. Snappy Storage Solutions (GoodHouseKeeping.com)

Day 27 Checklist:

- ☐ Take a "before" photo
- ☐ Remove and put away any items that belong in other rooms.
- ☐ Sort and declutter. Gather all craft supplies. Sort them by type (adhesives, papers, fabric, cutting implements, etc.), and by project.
  - *Keep only items that:*
    - You have used for a project in the last year
    - You enjoy working with and feel good about
    - You have enough of, to be used for a solidified future project (not scraps)
    - Can fit within a designated craft/storage area
  - *Do not keep items that:*
    - You are keeping out of guilt
    - Were used for a completed project and can't be used for a concrete project in the future
    - Are damaged or will not be used in the future
- ☐ Let go! Purge all items that do not fit into the keep category or those that cannot be sorted and stored in the given space. Discard broken items and box or bag other items for donation.
- ☐ Clean your crafting area. Wipe down shelves, cupboards, and drawers. Sweep, vacuum, and clean glass surfaces.
- ☐ Create functional storage solutions for all your craft supplies. Look on Pinterest or other resources within your own hobby genre for creative storage solution ideas that fit the needs for your particular passion.
- ☐ Label everything! Take the time to clearly label bins and storage containers, using labels or even a

Polaroid-type picture on the outside of each bin. Everything should have a designated place.

☐ Immediately toss or donate unwanted items.
☐ Take an "after" photo and share on Instagram, Facebook, Pinterest, or Twitter with the hashtag #LWSLClutterFree!

$\mathcal{D}ay$ 28: Control Center

Your family control or command center is the area where you track all your family happenings and post your weekly plan for your household. It is an invaluable tool for organizing yourself, your meals, your finances and the general running of your home--a physical dashboard to driving your life. If you don't yet have a control center, today is the day you will implement one!

Your control center should start with a magnetic whiteboard or chalkboard, as well as a bulletin board and a calendar. It should provide an at-a-glance view of your month, containing important scheduling and to-do items, including cleaning, organizing, meals, jobs and social obligations. For parents, it can help you remember piano lessons, soccer practice and gymnastics—and that on Thursday you are taking a meal to the neighbors with a new baby, so on Tuesday you need to remember to pick up supplies at the grocery store. Your control center is what will keep you on task. It will save you trips to the store, ensure you don't forget a birthday gift, and it will ease your mind so you don't have to worry about that "thing" hanging over you.

Your meal plan and ongoing grocery list should also be kept in your control center in order to avoid stress the stress of wondering what to make for dinner or not knowing if you have the ingredients on hand. Additionally, your control center should be the place you keep important phone numbers and instructions for babysitters or other household helpers.

While it does take some effort to get a control center set up and operational, it is not too difficult to maintain. The first of the month (or a few days before) is usually a good time to designate as your monthly Control Center Set-Up Day. Take a few hours and organize the Control Center. Make notes throughout the month of what works for you and change as needed.

Objective: A functional Family Control Center where you can organize a month's worth of cleaning, household tasks, meals, important events and social obligations.

Assess the current situation: How many members are in your household and who will use the Control Center? What room or task can you focus on each day? What major social obligations, visitors and events do you have in the next month? What are the important phone numbers you need to have at your fingertips and leave for the babysitter? What are your family's favorite meals and basic ingredients?

Assignment:

1. **Gather your essentials.** To create your control center you will need a magnetic clips, whiteboard or chalkboard, a bulletin board, magnetic clips, a calendar, and chalk or dry-erase markers.

2. **Create your control center.** Hang control center essentials in a central location in your home so that it is easy and convenient for all family members to reference it on a daily basis.

3. **Identify your players.** Make a list of each household member and assign them a color on the board.

4. **Plan meals.** Make a list of your family's favorite meals and basic ingredients for those meals. Calendar the meals on the chart.

5. **Create a cleaning schedule.** Use the tools found at www. LivingWellSpendingLess.com/cleaningschedule to create a cleaning schedule that works for you and your family. Plan a speed cleaning session for each day, or assign each room or area of your house to a different day, and add it to your calendar. Plan 15-20 minutes per day to start, if an hour seems too overwhelming at first.

6. **Fill in the calendar.** In the appropriate colors for each family member, add social obligations, extracurricular activities, appointments, tests, etc. Hang chalk or markers on or near the board, so it can be updated as needed.

7. **Create a contact sheet.** Gather and list important phone numbers and notes, and post them on the board.

CONTROL CENTER INSPIRATION

www.LivingWellSpendingLess.com

Entryway Inspiration

1. Midful Mornings Control (ContainerStore.com)
2. Cozy Corner Command Center (RealSimple.com)
3. Wall of Duty (RealSimple.com)
4. Family Command Center (BHG.com)
5. Daily System Solutions (PotteryBarn.com)

Day 28 Checklist:

☐ Take a "before" photo

☐ Gather your essentials. To create your control center you will need the following:
- magnetic clips
- whiteboard or chalkboard
- a bulletin board, magnetic clips
- a calendar, and chalk or dry-erase markers.

☐ Hang your control center items in a central location within your home so that it is easy for everyone in the family to reference it on a daily basis.

☐ Identify your players. Make a list of each household member and assign them a color on the board.

☐ Plan meals. Make a list of your family's favorite meals and basic ingredients for those meals. Calendar the meals on the chart.

☐ Create a cleaning schedule. Use the tools found at www.LivingWellSpendingLess.com/cleaningschedule to create a cleaning schedule that works for you and your family. Plan a speed cleaning session for each day, or assign each room or area of your house to a different day, and add it to your calendar.

☐ Fill in the calendar. In the appropriate colors for each family member, add social obligations, extracurricular activities, appointments, tests, etc. Hang chalk or markers on or near the board, so it can be updated as needed.

☐ Create a contact sheet. Gather and list important phone numbers and notes, and post them on the board.

☐ Clean your control center area. Wipe down shelves, cupboards, and drawers. Sweep, vacuum, and clean glass surfaces.

☐ Immediately toss or donate unwanted items.

☐ Take an "after" photo and share on Instagram, Facebook, Pinterest, or Twitter with the hashtag #LWSLClutterFree!

$\mathcal{D}ay$ 29: **Address Book**

In this digital era, many of us rely on our Google contacts, iPhone and Facebook to maintain our address book. With a simple click of a button or search we can have access to all the information—it's portable, it's easy to update, and it's right in our phones.

Unfortunately, unlike the paper address books of yesterday, having several contact lists mean that we often don't have all of the information stored in the same place. Facebook might alert you to birthdays, but there are those who are not on Facebook or don't share birthdays on social media. Google Contacts often maintains email addresses and updates, but may not have phone numbers. If you sync your contact list with your smart phone, you may then have some phone numbers, some email addresses, some birthdays and almost no one's street address.

The joy of sending and receiving mail is a tradition that should not be undervalued or lost. Despite the admonition to cut back on paper, sending a birthday card, thank you note or other message in the mail is still a very thoughtful gesture. It is vital to have an address book in order to do so.

I personally prefer to store all my contacts and addresses in an Excel spreadsheet. My husband and I usually update it once a year, as we prepare to send out our Christmas cards. However, if you prefer a paper address book, take an afternoon to copy the information into the book, and update it just as frequently.

A well-maintained address book can literally be your lifeline when you need to reach out to someone. Just a little time to complete it can be extremely valuable in the long run. Don't be afraid to declutter and eliminate old contacts from your address book as well. Focus on maintaining fewer acquaintances but more genuine friendships.

Objective: An updated and accessible address book that you maintain with complete contact information and birthdates.

Assess the current situation: Where do you currently keep all your contact information? What is your preferred and most easily accessed method? Do you regularly send Christmas cards or have a big event coming up that will require invitations?

Assignment:

1. **Gather your contacts.** Collect all of your current contact information from your various sources, such as Outlook, Google, Facebook, stacks of business cards, and paper address book.

2. **Merge your lists.** Transcribe or transfer all contact information to one source, such as an Excel spreadsheet, saving frequently.

3. **Update.** Make a list of addresses that need research or additional contact information that needs to be updated. Include birthdays, anniversaries and important milestones.

4. **Reach out.** Use this opportunity to reach out to some of those you've lost contact with and research their information.

5. **Maintain.** Commit to updating the information regularly.

Address Book

Name	Name
Address	Address
Cell #	Cell #
Work #	Work #
Home #	Home #
Email	Email
Name	Name
Address	Address
Cell #	Cell #
Work #	Work #
Home #	Home #
Email	Email
Name	Name
Address	Address
Cell #	Cell #
Work #	Work #
Home #	Home #
Email	Email
Name	Name
Address	Address
Cell #	Cell #
Work #	Work #
Home #	Home #
Email	Email

Address Book

Address Book Inspiration
Customized DIY Address Book (WordLabel.com)

Day 29 Checklist:

- ☐ Take a "before" photo
- ☐ Gather your contacts. Collect all of your current contact information from your various sources, such as Outlook, Google, Facebook, stacks of business cards, and paper address book.
- ☐ Merge your lists. Transcribe or transfer all contact information to one source, such as an Excel spreadsheet, saving frequently.
- ☐ Update. Make a list of addresses that need research or additional contact information that needs to be updated. Include birthdays, anniversaries and important milestones.
- ☐ Reach out. Use this opportunity to reach out to some of those you've lost contact with and research their information.
- ☐ Maintain. Commit to updating the information regularly.
- ☐ Immediately toss scraps of paper or business cards that have now been documented.
- ☐ Take an "after" photo and share on Instagram, Facebook, Pinterest, or Twitter with the hashtag #LWSLClutterFree!

$\mathcal{D}ay$ 30: Calendar and Schedule

The most successful and productive people keep close watch over their calendars and schedule. We can't always control everything, but with a carefully guarded calendar, we can plan and organize our time, increase our efficiency, and maintain our sanity.

Just like an address book, a calendar can come in many different forms—paper or digital, or even mobile. Some of us prefer to use different calendars for different activities—for example, the family calendar in your control center may not hold your business meetings and your office calendar may not reflect your upcoming anniversary or doctor's appointment.

It is important to find a method that works best for you and stick to it. The most effective calendar is, of course, one that you use and update regularly. If that means a Google calendar that syncs with your smartphone, great! If that means a paper calendar you keep in your pocketbook, fine! Simply use it and maximize it as a tool.

Regardless of what method you use to manage your calendar, it is important to realize that how you fill it depends on your ability to set limits and boundaries. The best calendar app in the world won't cure an overbooked schedule if the real problem is your inability to say no. Decluttering your schedule means figuring out what to cut out of your schedule, not what to add in.

Only say yes to the things that are most important to you, and ruthlessly cut out the rest. Practice the art of saying no graciously, and don't commit out of guilt or obligation if the task doesn't align with your priorities. If you do want to commit to something, calendar it—make time for it and stick to it.

Objective: A calendar to help you schedule tasks and manage time usage wisely.

Assess the current situation: How are you currently spending your time? What activities provide the most amount of stress? What could you cut out without guilt? What do you see as the most effective calendar method for you? How can you maximize the usage of that calendar?

Assignment:

1. **Decide on a calendar.** Will you use a paper planner? A wall calendar? Google calendar? An app? Pick one single calendar to plan your activities, then stick with it so nothing gets lost.

2. **Assess your priorities.** What are the things that are most important to you? These are the things that should take up the most time on your schedule.

3. **Clear out the unessential.** Immediately eliminate from your schedule anything that does not align with your priorities. Stop saying yes when you want to say know. Cancel appointments or activities that you don't actually need or want to keep.

4. **Make a list of the things you want and need to do**—be as specific as possible for each day. Gather all scraps of paper, such as notes or appointment cards into one central location so that they can be documented.

5. **Block out time on your calendar for each activity with an estimated time.** Build in free or empty time as buffers. Include any items that seem important like going to the gym, grocery shopping, driving your child to an appointment, and, of course "family time."

6. **Maintain and update.** At the end of each day, review your calendar, move any incomplete items forward and review time estimates and any previously expected events. Follow the calendar to help manage your time and commit to updating the information regularly.

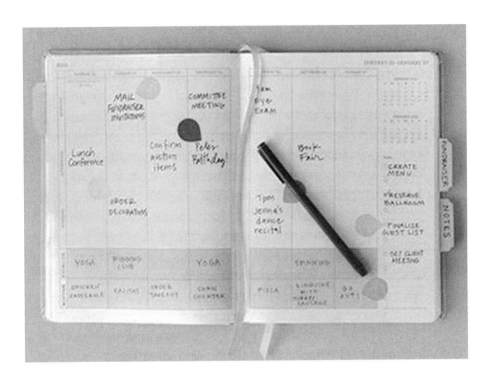

Calendar and Schedule Inspiration *(photos on right)*
Keep Your Busy Household On Track (Staples.com)

Day 30 Checklist:

- ☐ Take a "before" photo
- ☐ Decide on a calendar. Will you use a paper planner? A wall calendar? Google calendar? An app? Pick one single calendar to plan your activities, then stick with it so nothing gets lost.
- ☐ Assess your priorities. What are the things that are most important to you? These are the things that should take up the most time on your schedule.
- ☐ Clear out the unessential. Immediately eliminate from your schedule anything that does not align with your priorities. Stop saying yes when you want to say know. Cancel appointments or activities that you don't actually need or want to keep.
- ☐ Make a list of the things you want and need to do—be as specific as possible for each day. Gather all scraps of paper, such as notes or appointment cards into one central location so that they can be documented.
- ☐ Block out time on your calendar for each activity with an estimated time. Build in free or empty time as buffers. Include any items that seem important like going to the gym, grocery shopping, driving your child to an appointment, and, of course "family time."
- ☐ Maintain and update. At the end of each day, review your calendar, move any incomplete items forward and review time estimates and any previously expected events. Follow the calendar to help manage your time and commit to updating the information regularly.

☐ Immediately toss scraps of paper, appointment cards, and other items that have now been documented.

☐ Take an "after" photo and share on Instagram, Facebook, Pinterest, or Twitter with the hashtag #LWSLClutterFree!

Day 31: Clutter Free Forever

I've said it before, but I will say it again: the biggest problem and roadblock when it comes to living an organized life is not a lack of space, but **too much stuff.** Our modern lives lend themselves to clutter with the overabundance of materials, technology that is constantly changing, a culture of consumerism and the need to constantly have *more.*

We often struggle to manage our time and our households, and our health and relationships simply because of excess. Every now and then we just have to take a step back in order to stop the flow, prioritize our lives and think about the way we truly want to spend our time.

No one ever looked back on their life and wished they had more stuff to manage and take care of. Instead, most people tend to look back on their lives and wish they'd spent more time on their relationships with their families and strengthening their faith. They wish that they'd studied more, been more creative, and spent less time working hard to afford more.

I don't know about you, but I don't want to be one of those people who looks back at my life full of pretty things with nothing but regret.

Today marks the end of our thirty-one day challenge, but it is only the beginning of a clutter free life. To truly live clutter free forever, we have to commit, today and every day, to stay that way.

Adopting these four simple strategies from here on out can make all the difference in the world:

1. Stop the Flow

Just a simple trip to Target reminds us how easy it can be to mind-lessly fill our carts with things we don't need. Temptation is every-where, and for most of us, when like something, we buy it. What does it matter if we don't really *need* it? Our desire creates the need

Thus, the first step in living a clutter-free life is to commit to stop-ping the flow. We have to vigilantly guard against the sheer num-ber of things coming in. For me it has meant avoiding my favorite stores; for others it may mean avoiding the thrift stores or no more garage sale hopping. It means winning the mental battle and convincing yourself that what you have is already enough.

2. Ruthlessly Purge

Paring down the number of things you already have is the next phase of the battle, and luckily we have just spent an entire month decluttering our homes, which is a huge head start. Continue to give yourself permission to **only keep the things that are currently useful**, despite *who gave them to you* or *how much they cost*. This can be really hard, especially at first. That's where the ruthless part comes in.

As you continue to sort through your things, ask yourself these questions:

1. *Do we use it, wear it, or play with it? If it is clothes, does it still fit?*
2. *Is it in good working condition?*
3. *Does it enrich our lives in some way?*
4. *Does it have sentimental value?*
5. *Could someone else use it more?*

As you sort, it can be helpful to divide your things into four piles—things to keep, things to donate, things to throw away, and things to put elsewhere (such as a keepsake box items, seasonal storage, or things that belong in a different room). Once you've cleared an area and put away all the items that belong elsewhere, move on to the next area. Repeat. Repeat. Repeat.

3. Set Strict Limits

We live in a time of more excess and waste than ever before. We think nothing of a closet full of clothes, where our grandmothers and great-grandmothers only ever had a few dresses and a single pair of shoes to get them by. Holidays and birthdays are accompanied by piles of gifts rather than just one or two, while our kitchens and bathrooms are packed to the gills with gadgets, accessories, and products.

Our grandparents didn't have to set limits because they were already limited by their finances and by what was available. In an era where everything is available and affordable, **we have to be diligent about setting our own limits**. One way I did this was in my bedroom closet, where I limited my clothing to what would fit on forty hangers. Compared to the closets of a century ago, forty hangers is probably still a lot, but for me–and for most women today–getting rid of that many clothes was a pretty drastic change.

We also set some pretty strict limits when it comes to our kids and toys. After taking their toys away last year, we have tried to be very careful about the number of toys they have access to. This means limiting Christmas and birthday gifts and, when necessary, swapping out something they no longer play with when they do get something new.

4. Value Quality over Quantity

I think sometimes we have become so accustomed to the steady flow of cheaply-made junk that we forget that quality really does matter. Being incredibly selective, but then spending a little more to buy something that will stand the test of time is not only more frugal, but it is the way things simply used to be. At some point our standards lowered so much that we no longer think twice when a motor stops working after a year, or when our t-shirt gets a hole after just a few washings, or when another toy breaks after only being played with for a week.

When you *do* find yourself in need of something new, commit actively seeking out things that are well made from quality materials. Take the time to read reviews or to find things that are made locally rather than overseas. Choose long term value over short term savings.

Commit to rethinking consumerism as a family—build memories and experiences rather than accumulating "stuff." Spend a day doing an activity and bring nothing home but memories and strengthened family bonds.

Staying organized and committing to an organized life takes practice. It takes repetition. I suggest that you revisit your progress each month. Start at the top of this list and rework your way through. Focus on cleaning, tidying and revisiting the loose ends

Now that you've cleared the clutter, wouldn't it be nice to have a place to connect and collaborate with others, or to gather practical tips and accountability in a safe, warm, and encouraging atmosphere?

LWSLeveryday.com is that place.

Through a combination of an active community forum, inspiring interviews, LIVE Q&A sessions, and monthly access to limited-edition downloads, LWSL Everyday will encourage, empower, and inspire you to seek-and-find-the Good Life every single day.

As a member of LWSL Everyday, you will:

In joining this membership, you will:

- Get real-life accountability to help you set and achieve your financial and personal goals.
- Find new ideas for saving money and living well on a budget through inspiring behind-the-scenes interviews with your favorite authors.
- Gain exclusive access each month to beautifully designed, limited edition downloads.
- Connect with Ruth and get honest answers to your hardest questions in a monthly live webinar.

Your community is waiting.

Join us today at www.LWSLeveryday.com

each month. Keep it as an ongoing priority and you'll be amazed at how wonderful clutter-free can be.

And friends, that's it. The end of our month-long challenge and the beginning of your clutter-free life. Don't forget to continue to share your decluttering successes on social media with the hashtag #LWSLClutterFree, and be diligent and intentional about keeping your home, mind, and schedule clutter-free from here on out.

Here's to you, and a clutter-free life!